LPIC-1 102-500 V5 EXAM PREP: MASTER LINUX ADMIN WITH 6 PRACTICE TESTS

Realistic Practice Exams with Detailed Solutions for Success

Ghada Atef

To all aspiring Linux administrators,

May these practice exams illuminate your path, sharpen your skills, and lead you to triumph in the world of Linux.

With unwavering dedication,

Ghada Atef

"The journey of a thousand miles begins with a single step."

LAO TZU

CONTENTS

PREFACE

Welcome to the world of Linux administration! Whether you're a seasoned IT professional or just embarking on your journey, this book is your trusted companion for mastering the LPIC-1 102-500 V5 exam.

As you delve into the intricacies of Linux, you'll encounter challenges, triumphs, and countless lines of code. Fear not! My goal is to equip you with the knowledge, confidence, and practical skills needed to excel in the LPIC-1 certification.

Within these pages, you'll find **six meticulously crafted practice exams**—each a reflection of real-world scenarios. These exams aren't mere simulations; they're your stepping stones toward success. I've dissected every question, unraveled the complexities, and provided detailed solutions to guide you.

Remember, Linux isn't just an operating system; it's a philosophy—a community-driven force that empowers innovation. So, let's embark on this journey together. Whether you're navigating the command line or configuring network services, embrace the challenge, learn from mistakes, and celebrate victories.

May your Linux adventure be filled with discovery, growth, and the joy of mastering a powerful tool. Let's dive in!

GHADA ATEF

PROLOGUE

The digital world is constantly evolving, and the need for skilled Linux administrators is stronger than ever. Linux, renowned for its stability, security, and versatility, forms the backbone of countless systems, from personal computers to enterprise servers. Earning the LPIC-1 certification validates your foundational understanding of Linux administration and unlocks doors to fulfilling career opportunities in various industries.

This prologue serves as a stepping stone into the realm of Linux administration and the journey you're about to embark on. Imagine yourself confidently navigating the command line, managing users and groups, configuring file systems, and ensuring the smooth operation of Linux systems. This book equips you with the knowledge and practical skills to transform this vision into reality.

As you delve deeper into the chapters, remember that the path to mastering Linux administration is paved with dedication, perseverance, and a thirst for knowledge. Embrace the challenges, celebrate your victories, and never stop learning. This book is your companion on this rewarding adventure, offering guidance, support, and the tools you need to succeed.

Prepare to unlock your potential, conquer the LPIC-1 exam, and embark on a rewarding career as a Linux administrator.

The adventure begins now!

CONTACT ME

Thank you for embarking on this Linux journey with *LPIC-1 102-500 V5 Exam Prep*. If you have questions, feedback, or need assistance, feel free to reach out!

Email: linux.expert.eg@gmail.com

Please note that I aim to respond within **72 hours**. Your inquiries are valuable, and I appreciate your patience.

Let's continue our exploration of Linux together!

GHADA ATEF

PRACTICE TEST ONE - LPIC-1 EXAM 102 VERSION: 5.0

90 questions | 2 hours | 90% correct required to pass

The LPIC-1 Exam 102 Version: 5.0 Practice Test is a comprehensive resource designed to prepare you for the LPIC-1 (Linux Professional Institute Certification) Exam 102. It includes practice questions that mimic the format and content of the actual test. Each **Question** comes with a detailed **Explanation** to help you understand the concepts better. This practice test is an excellent tool to harness the power of Linux and achieve LPIC-1 certification.

Note

The 102 actual exam is a 90-minute exam with 60 multiple-choice and fill-in-the-blank questions.

Question 1:

What is the primary purpose of startup scripts in the Linux shell environment?

A) To execute user commands.

B) To customize the session's environment.

(Correct)

C) To manage system processes.

D) To facilitate file operations.

Explanation

Startup scripts in the Linux shell environment are used to customize the session's environment by setting variables, aliases, and functions according to user preferences.

Question 2:

Which shell is the de facto standard for the majority of Linux distributions?

A) Korn Shell (ksh)

B) C Shell (csh)

C) Bourne Again Shell (Bash)

(Correct)

D) Z Shell (zsh)

Explanation

Bash is the default shell for most Linux distributions and is widely used due to its extensive features and compatibility.

Question 3:

Which file sets system-wide environment variables for login shells in Linux?

A) /etc/bash.bashrc

B) /etc/profile

(Correct)

C) ~/.bashrc

D) ~/.bash_profile

Explanation

The /etc/profile file is the system-wide .profile file for login shells, which sets environment variables for all users upon login.

Question 4:

What command can be used to determine the type of shell currently in use?

A) echo $SHELL

B) echo $0

(Correct)

C) uname -s

D) ps aux | grep shell

Explanation

The command "echo $0" prints the name of the shell currently in use, indicating whether it's an interactive login shell, an interactive non-login shell, or a non-interactive shell.

Question 5:

Which startup file is executed by non-interactive non-login

shells?

A) ~/.profile

B) /etc/profile

C) ~/.bashrc

D) None of the above

(Correct)

Explanation

Non-interactive non-login shells, such as scripts, do not execute any of the typical startup files like ~/.profile or /etc/profile. Instead, they look for the environment variable BASH_ENV and execute the file specified by its value.

Question 6:

How can a user ensure that changes made to a startup file take effect without rebooting?

A) Log out and log back in.

B) Restart the shell.

C) Use the "source" or "." command.

(Correct)

D) Use the "exec" command.

Explanation

The "source" or "." command is used to execute a file within the current shell session, allowing changes made to the file to take effect immediately without requiring a reboot or shell restart.

Question 7:

Which directory serves as a template for the file system structure of new user accounts in Linux?

A) /etc/skel

(Correct)

B) /var/user

C) /home/template

D) /usr/default

Explanation

The /etc/skel directory contains files and directories that are copied into the home directory of new user accounts, serving as a template for their initial environment.

Question 8:

Which command, when used without any additional options or parameters, can create a new user account in Linux and populate it with files from the skel directory?

A) useradd

B) adduser

(Correct)

C) createuser

D) newuser

Explanation

The "adduser" command is used to create a new user account

in Linux and automatically populate its home directory with files from the /etc/skel directory.

Question 9:

Which command is used to change the mode bits of a file to make it executable?

A) chmod

(Correct)

B) chown

C) chgrp

D) chmodx

Explanation

The "chmod" command is used to change the permissions of a file or directory in Linux, including making it executable by adding the execute permission bit.

Question 10:

What is the purpose of sourcing a file in the shell environment?

A) To display its contents.

B) To delete it from the system.

C) To execute its commands within the current shell session.

(Correct)

D) To rename it.

Explanation

Sourcing a file in the shell environment means executing its commands within the current shell session, allowing any changes made by the file to take effect immediately.

Question 11:

Which startup file is executed by interactive non-login shells at the local level for Bash?

A) /etc/profile

B) /etc/bash.bashrc

C) ~/.profile

D) ~/.bashrc

(Correct)

Explanation

The ~/.bashrc file is executed by interactive non-login shells at the local level for Bash. It is typically used to set shell options, define functions, and create aliases.

Question 12:

What command can be used to list all currently running processes containing the word "bash" in their command line?

A) ps -e | grep bash

B) ps aux | grep bash

(Correct)

C) top | grep bash

D) pgrep bash

Explanation

The "ps aux | grep bash" command lists all currently running processes and filters out those containing the word "bash" in their command line using the grep command.

Question 13:

Study how the shells have been started under the column "Shell Started with…" and verify whether the provided information is True or False:

Shell Started with…	Interactive?	Login?	Result of echo $0
`sudo ssh user2@machine2`	No	Yes	`-bash`
`Ctrl + Alt + F2`	Yes	Yes	`tty2`
`su - user2`	Yes	Yes	`-bash`
`gnome-terminal`	Yes	No	`bash`
A regular user uses `konsole` to start an instance of `sakura`	Yes	No	`sakura`
A script named `test.sh` containing the command `echo $0`	No	No	`-bash`

A) True

B) False

(Correct)

Explanation:

1. sudo ssh user2@machine2: This command initiates an interactive login shell on machine2 as user2. The -bash output of echo $0 indicates that the shell is a bash shell, which is correct.

2. Ctrl + Alt + F2: This key combination switches to a new virtual console in Linux. It starts an interactive login shell, and -bash is the correct output of echo $0.

3. su - user2: This command initiates a new login shell as user2. It's interactive and the -bash output of echo $0 indicates that the shell is a bash shell.

4. gnome-terminal: This command opens a new terminal window. It's an interactive non-login shell, and bash is the correct output of echo $0.

5. A regular user uses konsole to start an instance of sakura: This scenario describes a user starting an instance of sakura terminal emulator in konsole. It's an interactive non-login shell, and /bin/bash is the correct output of echo $0.

6. A script named test.sh containing the command echo $0: When a script is run, it starts a non-interactive non-login shell. The ./test.sh is the output of echo $0.

Question 14:

What is the purpose of the shebang line in a shell script?

A) It comments out the script to disable execution.

B) It specifies the interpreter to execute the script.

(Correct)

C) It defines the location of the script file.

D) It sets environment variables for the script.

Explanation

The shebang line (`#!/bin/bash`) at the beginning of a script specifies the interpreter (in this case, `/bin/bash`) that should be used to execute the script.

Question 15:

Which command is used to change the permissions of a script file to make it executable?

A) `exec`

B) `chmod`

(Correct)

C) `chown`

D) `perm`

Explanation

The `chmod` command is used to change file permissions. Adding the execute permission is done with `chmod +x`.

Question 16:

What does the `$?` variable store after executing a script?

A) The script's content

B) The script's exit status code

(Correct)

C) The script's interpreter path

D) The script's owner information

Explanation

After executing a script, the `$?` variable stores the exit status code of the last executed command or script.

Question 17:

How can you read user input in a shell script?

A) Using the `input` command

B) Using the `get` command

C) Using the `read` command

(Correct)

D) Using the `echo` command

Explanation

The `read` command is used to read input from the user within a shell script.

Question 18:

Which operator is used for logical AND in shell script conditional statements?

A) `&&`

(Correct)

B) `||`

C) `&`

D) `|`

Explanation

In shell script conditional statements, `&&` is used for logical AND, meaning that the second command is executed only if the first command succeeds.

Question 19:

What is the purpose of the `printf` command in shell scripting?

A) To print formatted output

(Correct)

B) To print text to the console

C) To read user input

D) To execute commands

Explanation

The `printf` command is used to print formatted output, allowing for precise control over the appearance of the output.

Question 20:

Which parameter stores the name of the script file being executed?

A) `$0`

(Correct)

B) `$1`

C) `$?`

D) `` `$@` ``

Explanation

The `` `$0` `` parameter stores the name of the script file being executed.

Question 21:

What is the primary version of the X protocol used in modern Linux distributions?

A) X.org version 10

B) X.org version 9

C) X.org version 11

(Correct)

D) X.org version 8

Explanation

X.org version 11, commonly referred to as X11, is the primary version of the X protocol used in modern Linux distributions.

Question 22:

Which component of the X Window System informs the X server about the window location and size on a computer screen?

A) Window manager

B) Display manager

C) X client

(Correct)

D) Desktop environment

Explanation

The X client component of the X Window System informs the X server about the window location and size on a computer screen.

Question 23:

What is the primary responsibility of a display manager in the X Window System?

A) Rendering graphics

B) Managing access to the X server

C) Handling device input

D) Providing a graphical login interface

(Correct)

Explanation

A display manager provides a graphical login interface to the X Window System.

Question 24:

Which component of a desktop environment is responsible for controlling window placement and decorations?

A) File manager

B) Window manager

(Correct)

C) Taskbar

D) Application launcher

Explanation

The window manager controls window placement and decorations, such as adding title bars and control buttons to windows, and managing the switching between open windows.

Question 25:

Which desktop environment is known for its resource efficiency and modular structure?

A) KDE

B) Gnome

C) Xfce

(Correct)

D) LXDE

Explanation

Xfce is known for being aesthetically pleasing while consuming fewer machine resources compared to other desktop environments. Its structure is highly modularized, allowing users to activate and deactivate components according to their needs and preferences.

Question 26:

Which desktop environment is associated with the KDE Plasma version?

A) Gnome

B) Xfce

C) KDE

(Correct)

D) LXDE

Explanation

KDE Plasma is the latest version of the KDE desktop environment, known for its use of the Qt library and a plethora of original applications.

Question 27:

Where can accessibility settings typically be customized in major Linux distributions?

A) In the command line interface only

B) In the display settings

C) In the settings manager of the desktop environment

(Correct)

D) In the system BIOS

Explanation

Accessibility settings can typically be customized in the settings manager of the desktop environment provided by major Linux distributions.

Question 28:

Which desktop environment provides the Universal Access module for configuring accessibility settings?

A) KDE

B) Xfce

C) Gnome

(Correct)

D) LXDE

Explanation

Gnome provides the Universal Access module for configuring accessibility settings.

Question 29:

What feature, found in both Gnome and KDE, allows users to type keyboard shortcuts one key at a time, particularly helpful for users with mobility difficulties?

A) Sticky keys

(Correct)

B) Slow keys

C) Mouse keys

D) Bounce keys

Explanation

Sticky keys allow users to type keyboard shortcuts one key at a time, particularly helpful for users with mobility difficulties. This feature is found in both Gnome and KDE.

Question 30:

What command is used to add a new user account in Linux?

A) `adduser`

B) `newuser`

C) `usercreate`

D) `useradd`

(Correct)

Explanation

The `useradd` command is used to add a new user account in Linux systems.

Question 31:

Which file contains encrypted user passwords in Linux?

A) /etc/passwd

B) /etc/group

C) /etc/shadow

(Correct)

D) /etc/gshadow

Explanation

The `/etc/shadow` file contains encrypted user passwords in Linux.

Question 32:

What command is used to modify a user account in Linux?

A) `usermodify`

B) `moduser`

C) `usermod`

(Correct)

D) `edituser`

Explanation

The `usermod` command is used to modify a user account in Linux.

Question 33:

Which option of the `usermod` command is used to change the login shell of a user account?

A) -s

(Correct)

B) -l

C) -e

D) -c

Explanation

The `-s` option of the `usermod` command is used to change the login shell of a user account.

Question 34:

What command is used to delete a user account in Linux?

A) `deleteuser`

B) `removeuser`

C) `userdel`

(Correct)

D) `deluser`

Explanation

The `userdel` command is used to delete a user account in Linux.

Question 35:

Which file contains basic information about groups in Linux?

A) /etc/passwd

B) /etc/group

(Correct)

C) /etc/shadow

D) /etc/gshadow

Explanation

The `/etc/group` file contains basic information about groups in Linux.

Question 36:

What is the purpose of cron in Linux system administration?

A) To schedule one-time tasks at a specific time.

B) To manage system services and daemons.

C) To automate periodic job scheduling.

(Correct)

D) To control user access to system resources.

Explanation

Cron is used to schedule recurring tasks or jobs at specific intervals.

Question 37:

Which command is used to edit a user's crontab file?

A) cronedit

B) crontab -e

(Correct)

C) editcron

D) crontab edit

Explanation

The crontab -e command is used to edit a user's crontab file.

Question 38:

Where are system crontab files located in a Linux system?

A) /var/cron

B) /etc/cron

(Correct)

C) /var/spool/cron

D) /etc

Explanation

System crontab files are located in the /etc/cron directory.

Question 39:

Which of the following is NOT a valid time specification in cron?

A) 0 0 * * *

B) 30 12 * * 1-5

C) 0 25 * * *

(Correct)

D) */5 * * * *

Explanation

The minute field only accepts values from 0 to 59, so 25 is not a valid value.

Question 40:

What is the purpose of the at command in Linux?

A) To schedule one-time tasks at a specific time.

(Correct)

B) To automate periodic job scheduling.

C) To manage system services and daemons.

D) To edit cron jobs for individual users.

Explanation

The at command is used for one-time task scheduling.

Question 41:

Which command is used to list pending at jobs for a user?

A) listat

B) atlist

C) atq

(Correct)

D) atlist -u

Explanation

The atq command lists pending at jobs for a user.

Question 42:

What is the purpose of configuring locale settings and environment variables in a Linux system?

A) To improve system security

B) To enhance user experience and ensure correct time and language settings

(Correct)

C) To reduce system resource usage

D) To optimize network performance

Explanation

Configuring locale settings and environment variables is essential for customizing language, time zone, and character encoding settings in a Linux system, improving user experience and ensuring accurate time and language representation.

Question 43:

Which file contains the default time zone for the system in Linux?

A) /etc/timezone

(Correct)

B) /etc/localtime

C) /usr/share/zoneinfo/

D) /var/lib/timezone

Explanation

The default time zone for the system is stored in the file /etc/timezone, which can contain either the zone's full descriptive name or offset.

Question 44:

What command is used to interactively select the appropriate time zone in a Linux system?

A) timedatectl

B) date

C) tzselect

(Correct)

D) locale

Explanation

The tzselect command offers an interactive method to guide the user towards selecting the correct time zone definition for their location.

Question 45:

Which command can be used to display the current system time in Linux?

A) time

B) clock

C) date

(Correct)

D) datetime

Explanation

The `date` command is used to display the current system time in Linux.

Question 46:

What is the default time zone used for the system clock in Linux?

A) UTC

(Correct)

B) PST

C) EST

D) GMT

Explanation

The default time zone for the system clock in Linux is Coordinated Universal Time (UTC).

Question 47:

Which command is used to view the time maintained on the hardware clock in Linux?

A) rtc

B) systime

C) hwclock

(Correct)

D) clocksync

Explanation

The `hwclock` command is used to view and manage the hardware clock in Linux.

Question 48:

What is the primary purpose of system logging in Linux?

A) To monitor network bandwidth

B) To keep track of system and network events

(Correct)

C) To optimize CPU usage

D) To manage disk space

Explanation

System logging in Linux is crucial for keeping track of various system and network events, including authentication processes, service errors, and more. It helps in troubleshooting, security monitoring, and system analysis.

Question 49:

Which logging facility is commonly used in modern GNU/ Linux distributions?

A) syslog-ng

B) syslog

C) rsyslog

(Correct)

D) systemd-journald

Explanation

rsyslog is the most commonly used logging facility in modern GNU/Linux distributions due to its advanced features and reliability.

Question 50:

Which file contains centralized logs for practically all captured logs by rsyslogd?

A) /var/log/messages

B) /var/log/syslog

(Correct)

C) /var/log/auth.log

D) /var/log/debug

Explanation

The /var/log/syslog file typically contains centralized logs for practically all captured logs by rsyslogd.

Question 51:

What command is used to read the last lines of a log file in real-time?

A) head

B) zless

C) tail

(Correct)

D) grep

Explanation

The tail command is used to display the last few lines of a file, and with the '-f' option, it can be used to follow the growth of a log file in real-time.

Question 52:

What is the purpose of the logger command in Linux?

A) To compress log files

B) To rotate log files

C) To manually enter messages into the system log

(Correct)

D) To delete log files

Explanation

The logger command is used to manually enter messages into the system log, allowing users to add custom messages or events for logging purposes.

Question 53:

Which directive in the logrotate configuration file specifies the number of weeks worth of backlogs to keep?

A) daily

B) rotate

(Correct)

C) weekly

D) compress

Explanation

The 'rotate' directive in the logrotate configuration file specifies the number of log files to keep before rotating them.

Question 54:

What is the primary function of a Mail Transfer Agent (MTA) in a Unix-like operating system?

A) Storing email messages in individual inboxes

B) Forwarding messages between local and remote users

(Correct)

C) Authenticating users for remote email access

D) Filtering spam and malicious emails

Explanation

MTAs are responsible for collecting, forwarding, and delivering email messages between local user accounts as well as remote user accounts.

Question 55:

Which protocol is commonly used by MTAs to transfer email messages over the network?

A) FTP

B) SMTP

(Correct)

C) HTTP

D) SSH

Explanation

SMTP (Simple Mail Transfer Protocol) is the standard protocol used by MTAs for sending and receiving email messages over the Internet.

Question 56:

What is the primary configuration file for the CUPS service?

A) /etc/cups/printers.conf

B) /etc/printcap

C) /etc/cups/cupsd.conf

(Correct)

D) /var/log/cups/access_log

Explanation

The primary configuration file for the CUPS service is / etc/cups/cupsd.conf, which contains settings for controlling access to print queues, enabling the web interface, and configuring logging levels.

Question 57:

Which command is used to install and remove printers and printer classes in CUPS?

A) lpstat

B) lpadmin

(Correct)

C) lpr

D) lpq

Explanation

The lpadmin command is used to install and remove printers and printer classes in CUPS.

Question 58:

What is the default network port for accessing the CUPS web interface?

A) 80/TCP

B) 443/TCP

C) 631/TCP

(Correct)

D) 8080/TCP

Explanation

The default network port for accessing the CUPS web interface is 631/TCP.

Question 59:

What is the purpose of a network mask (netmask) in conjunction with an IP address?

A) To identify the default gateway

B) To determine the network and host portions of an IP address

(Correct)

C) To encrypt data transmitted over the network

D) To assign a unique identifier to each device on the network

Explanation

A network mask is used to identify which portion of an IP address is the network portion and which portion is the host portion.

Question 60:

Which of the following is a valid IPv4 address class?

A) Class D: 224.0.0.0 - 239.255.255.255

B) Class E: 240.0.0.0 - 255.255.255.255

C) Class B: 128.0.0.0 - 191.255.255.255

(Correct)

D) Class C: 192.0.0.0 - 223.255.255.255

Explanation

Class B addresses have the first octet range from 128 to 191.

Question 61:

Which of the following is an example of a private IP address?

A) 192.168.10.1

(Correct)

B) 172.33.44.55

C) 200.100.50.25

D) 185.20.15.10

Explanation

The range of IP addresses 192.168.0.0/16 is reserved for private networks.

Question 62:

What is the primary purpose of CIDR notation?

A) To indicate the class of an IP address

B) To specify the number of hosts on a network

C) To simplify representation of network prefixes

(Correct)

D) To identify multicast addresses

Explanation

CIDR notation represents the network prefix and the number of significant bits in the mask.

Question 63:

GHADAATEF

Which of the following ports is commonly associated with the HTTPS service?

A) 21

B) 80

C) 443

(Correct)

D) 25

Explanation

HTTPS typically uses port 443 for secure communication.

Question 64:

Which command can be used to list network interfaces in a Linux system?

A) netstat

B) ifconfig

C) ip

(Correct)

D) arp

Explanation

The `ip` command is used to display and manipulate routing, devices, policy routing, and tunnels in a Linux system.

Question 65:

What is the purpose of the `/etc/hostname` file in Linux?

A) It stores the DNS server configuration.

B) It contains the list of network interfaces.

C) It specifies the static hostname of the system.

(Correct)

D) It stores DHCP lease information.

Explanation

The `/etc/hostname` file stores the static hostname of the system.

Question 66:

Which command is used to activate a network interface defined in the `/etc/network/interfaces` file?

A) ifup

(Correct)

B) ifconfig

C) ipconfig

D) ifdown

Explanation

The `ifup` command is used to bring up a network interface based on its configuration in the `/etc/network/interfaces` file.

Question 67:

What is the naming convention for Ethernet interfaces in recent Linux systems?

A) eth0, eth1, etc.

B) enp3s5, ens1, etc.

(Correct)

C) wlan0, wlan1, etc.

D) ib0, ib1, etc.

Explanation

Recent Linux systems use the naming convention where Ethernet interfaces start with prefixes like `en` followed by other identifiers.

Question 68:

Which command can be used to set the hostname in Linux?

A) hostnamectl

(Correct)

B) hostconfig

C) hostnamemod

D) sysctl

Explanation

The `hostnamectl` command is used to set or view the hostname in Linux systems.

Question 69:

In the `/etc/hosts` file, what is the purpose of the line `127.0.0.1 localhost`?

A) It defines the DNS server IP address.

B) It associates the IP address 127.0.0.1 with the hostname localhost.

(Correct)

C) It defines the default gateway IP address.

D) It defines the loopback interface.

Explanation

This line in the `/etc/hosts` file associates the IP address 127.0.0.1 with the hostname localhost, which is used for loopback testing.

Question 70:

Which file is responsible for configuring the resolver in Linux?

A) /etc/resolv.conf

(Correct)

B) /etc/hostname

C) /etc/hosts

D) /etc/nsswitch.conf

Explanation

The `/etc/resolv.conf` file is responsible for configuring the resolver in Linux, specifying DNS server information.

Question 71:

What is the purpose of the `auto` keyword in the `/etc/network/interfaces` file?

A) It specifies the DHCP configuration.

B) It identifies the physical interfaces to be brought up automatically during boot.

(Correct)

C) It sets the hostname of the system.

D) It defines the loopback interface.

Explanation

The `auto` keyword in the `/etc/network/interfaces` file identifies the physical interfaces to be brought up automatically during boot.

Question 72:

Which command is used to manually configure network interfaces and review their states in modern Linux distributions?

A) ifconfig

B) ip

(Correct)

C) netstat

D) route

Explanation

The ip command is the modern and versatile utility used to configure network interfaces and review their states in modern Linux distributions.

Question 73:

What is the purpose of the `ping` command in Linux

networking?

A) To view the routing table

B) To trace the route a packet takes to a destination

C) To send ICMP echo requests to test network connectivity

(Correct)

D) To set up arbitrary TCP or UDP connections

Explanation

The `ping` command is used to send ICMP echo requests to a specified destination address to test network connectivity.

Question 74:

How can you view the routing table in Linux using the `ip` command?

A) ip show routes

B) ip route

(Correct)

C) ip config

D) ip routing

Explanation

The `ip route` command is used to view the routing table in Linux using the `ip` command.

Question 75:

Which command is used to trace the route a packet takes to a destination in Linux?

A) ping

B) traceroute

(Correct)

C) netcat

D) tracepath

Explanation

The `traceroute` command is used to trace the route a packet takes to a destination in Linux.

Question 76:

What is the purpose of the `nc` command in Linux networking?

A) To view current network connections

B) To trace the maximum transmission unit (MTU) along a path

C) To send ICMP echo requests

D) To send or receive arbitrary data over TCP or UDP connections

(Correct)

Explanation

The `nc` command, also known as netcat, is used to send or receive arbitrary data over TCP or UDP connections in Linux.

Question 77:

Which command is used to view the status of current listeners and connections in Linux networking?

A) ping

B) netstat

(Correct)

C) traceroute

D) route

Explanation

The `netstat` command is used to view the status of current listeners and connections in Linux networking.

Question 78:

What is the primary function of the /etc/nsswitch.conf file in Linux?

A) Configuring DNS servers

B) Configuring local name resolution

(Correct)

C) Configuring network interfaces

D) Configuring firewall rules

Explanation

The /etc/nsswitch.conf file is used to configure how the system resolves various types of names, including host names.

Question 79:

Which DNS record class is typically used for internet addresses using the TCP/IP stack?

A) IN

(Correct)

B) HS

C) CH

D) MX

Explanation

The IN (Internet) class is used for internet addresses using the TCP/IP stack.

Question 80:

What special permission bit allows a file to be executed with the privileges of the file's owner?

A) SGID

B) SUID

(Correct)

C) Sticky bit

D) Execute bit

Explanation

The SUID (Set User ID) bit allows a file to be executed with the privileges of the file's owner.

Question 81:

Which command is used to change a user's password aging information?

A) `passwd`

B) `chage`

(Correct)

C) `usermod`

D) `chpasswd`

Explanation

The `chage` command is used to change a user's password aging information, such as minimum and maximum password age.

Question 82:

Which command is used to list open files on a Linux system?

A) `ls`

B) `lsof`

(Correct)

C) `fuser`

D) `netstat`

Explanation

The `lsof` command stands for "list open files" and is used to list open files and processes.

Question 83:

What file stores basic user account data, including login name, userid, groupid, and default shell?

A) /etc/passwd

(Correct)

B) /etc/shadow

C) /etc/xinetd.conf

D) /etc/inittab

Explanation

The /etc/passwd file contains basic user account information.

Question 84:

In modern systems, where are passwords stored instead of in the /etc/passwd file?

A) /etc/shadow

(Correct)

B) /etc/passwords

C) /etc/security

D) /etc/auth

Explanation

Passwords are stored in the /etc/shadow file in modern systems, while /etc/passwd contains other user account information.

Question 85:

Which command is used to change a user's password?

A) passchange

B) passwd

(Correct)

C) chpasswd

D) userpasswd

Explanation

The passwd command is used to change a user's password in Linux.

Question 86:

What is the main purpose of using the SSH (Secure Shell) protocol?

A) To authenticate users with passwords

B) To transmit data over unencrypted connections

C) To establish secure remote connections

(Correct)

D) To facilitate file transfers using FTP

Explanation

The SSH protocol is designed to provide secure remote access and communication between systems by encrypting data transmission.

Question 87:

Which command is used to establish a remote SSH session?

A) ssh-agent

B) ssh-keygen

C) ssh-add

D) ssh

(Correct)

Explanation

The `ssh` command is used to initiate a remote SSH session by specifying the user and hostname/IP address of the remote machine.

Question 88:

What is the purpose of the `known_hosts` file in SSH?

A) To store private SSH keys

B) To store public SSH keys

C) To store known IP addresses of remote hosts

D) To store fingerprints of known host public keys

(Correct)

Explanation

The `known_hosts` file stores the fingerprints of known host public keys for authentication during SSH connections.

Question 89:

Which key-based authentication method adds an extra layer of security by requiring a passphrase?

A) RSA

(Correct)

B) DSA

C) ecdsa

D) ed25519

Explanation

When using RSA key-based authentication, a passphrase can be added for an extra layer of security, which is recommended.

Question 90:

What is the purpose of the `ssh-agent` command?

A) To generate SSH key pairs

B) To add SSH public keys to authorized hosts

C) To authenticate SSH connections with passwords

D) To manage SSH private keys

(Correct)

Explanation

The `ssh-agent` command is used to manage SSH private keys, holding them in memory for authentication during SSH connections.

PRACTICE TEST TWO - LPIC-1 EXAM 102 VERSION: 5.0

90 questions | 2 hours | 90% correct required to pass

The LPIC-1 Exam 102 Version: 5.0 Practice Test is a comprehensive resource designed to prepare you for the LPIC-1 (Linux Professional Institute Certification) Exam 102. It includes practice questions that mimic the format and content of the actual test. Each **Question** comes with a detailed **Explanation** to help you understand the concepts better. This practice test is an excellent tool to harness the power of Linux and achieve LPIC-1 certification.

Note

The 102 actual exam is a 90-minute exam with 60 multiple-choice and fill-in-the-blank questions.

Question 1:

Check whether the provided information is True or False:

The su and sudo commands to launch the specified shell:

1. Interactive-login shell as user2:

su: su - user2 (True)

sudo: sudo -i -u user2 (True)

2. Interactive login shell as root:

su: su - or su - root (True)

sudo: sudo -i (True)

3. Interactive non-login shell as root:

su: su root (False)

sudo: sudo -s or sudo bash (True)

4. Interactive non-login shell as user2:

su: su user2 (True)

sudo: sudo -u user2 (True)

A) True

(Correct)

B) False

Explanation:

1. Interactive-login shell as user2:

su: su - user2: True. The - option initializes an interactive login shell for user2.

sudo: sudo -i -u user2: True. The -i option initializes an interactive login shell and -u specifies user2.

2. Interactive login shell as root:

su: *su - or su - root: True.* Either command initializes an interactive login shell for root.

sudo: *sudo -i: True.* The -i option initializes an interactive login shell as root.

3. Interactive non-login shell as root:

su: *su root: False.* Without the - option, su launches a non-login shell. The username root doesn't affect the login type.

sudo: *sudo -s or sudo bash:* True. Both commands start an interactive non-login shell as root. -s for sudo explicitly specifies a shell, and sudo bash directly calls the Bash shell.

4. Interactive non-login shell as user2:

su: *su user2: True.* Without the - option, su launches a non-login shell as user2.

sudo: *sudo -u user2: True.* The -u option specifies user2 for the command to be run.

Understanding the options and parameters of su and sudo commands is essential for managing user sessions and executing commands with elevated privileges. The -i option initializes an interactive login shell, while -s (for sudo) or specifying a shell directly (like sudo bash) initializes an interactive non-login shell. The -u option specifies the user for whom the command should be executed.

Question 2:

Check whether the provided information is True or False:

Startup files get read when the shell under "Shell Type" is started:

Shell Type	/etc/profile	/etc/bash.bashrc	~/.profile	~/.bashrc
Interactive-login shell as user2	Yes	No	Yes	No
Interactive login shell as root	Yes	No	No	Yes
Interactive non-login shell as root	No	Yes	No	Yes
Interactive non-login shell as user2	No	Yes	Yes	Yes

A) True

B) False

(Correct)

Explanation:

1. Interactive-login shell as user2:

/etc/profile: Yes. This file is sourced for interactive login shells for global environment settings.

/etc/bash.bashrc: Yes.

~/.profile: Yes. User-specific settings are usually configured in

this file for interactive login shells.

~/.bashrc: Yes. This file is not sourced for interactive login shells.

2. Interactive login shell as root:

/etc/profile: Yes. It's sourced for interactive login shells, including when root logs in.

/etc/bash.bashrc: Yes.

~/.profile: No. Typically, root doesn't have a user-specific profile file.

~/.bashrc: No. This file is typically sourced for interactive non-login shells, which include opening a new terminal window.

3. Interactive non-login shell as root:

/etc/profile: No. This file is not sourced for interactive non-login shells.

/etc/bash.bashrc: Yes. This file is typically sourced for interactive non-login shells to set up the user environment.

~/.profile: No. Similar to the previous case, root usually doesn't have a user-specific profile file.

~/.bashrc: No.

4. Interactive non-login shell as user2:

/etc/profile: No. This file is not sourced for interactive non-login shells.

/etc/bash.bashrc: Yes. It's sourced for interactive non-login shells.

~/.profile: No.

~/.bashrc: Yes. This file is sourced for interactive non-login

shells.

Understanding which startup files are read for different types of shells is crucial for customizing the shell environment and executing commands appropriately upon shell startup. The files in /etc directory are system-wide configurations, while ~ represents the user's home directory.

Question 3:

In Bash, we can write a simple Hello world! function by including the following code in an empty file:

```
function hello() {
echo "Hello world!"
}
```

1. What should we do next to make the function available to the shell?

A) Save the file as .bashrc in the home directory.

B) Save the file as .bash_profile in the home directory.

C) Source the file in the terminal or restart the shell.

D) Execute the file with bash.

2. Once it is available to the current shell, how would you invoke it?

A) Call `hello` in the terminal.

B) Execute the script file.

C) Type `./hello` in the terminal.

D) Type `source hello` in the terminal.

3. To automate things, in what file would you put the function

and its invocation so that it gets executed when user2 opens a terminal from an X Window session? What type of shell is it?

A) .bash_profile, interactive shell

B) .bashrc, interactive shell

C) .bash_profile, non-interactive shell

D) .bashrc, non-interactive shell

4. In what file would you put the function and its invocation so that it is run when root launches a new interactive shell irrespective of whether it is login or not?

A) .bash_profile

B) .bashrc

C) /etc/bash.bashrc

D) /etc/profile

1. C), 2. A), 3. A), 4. B)

(Correct)

1. A), 2. A), 3. A), 4. B)

1. C), 2. B), 3. A), 4. B)

1. C), 2. A), 3. D), 4. B)

Explanation

Answer: 1. C) Source the file in the terminal or restart the shell.

To make the function available, the file needs to be sourced in the terminal or the shell needs to be restarted.

Answer: 2. A) Call `hello` in the terminal.

Once the function is available, you can invoke it by simply typing `hello` in the terminal.

Answer: 3. A) .bash_profile, interactive shell

`.bash_profile` is sourced for login shells, and since opening a terminal from an X Window session involves logging in, it's the appropriate file. The shell is interactive.

Answer: 4. B) .bashrc

`.bashrc` is sourced for non-login interactive shells, which covers scenarios where root launches a new interactive shell.

Question 4:

Have a look at the following basic, Hello world! bash script:

```
#!/bin/bash

#hello_world: a simple bash script to discuss interaction in scripts.

echo "Hello world!"
```

1. Suppose we make the script executable and run it. Would that be an interactive script? Why?

A) Yes, because it prompts the user for input.

B) No, because it doesn't interact with the user.

C) Yes, because it interacts with the environment.

D) No, because it's not run in a terminal.

2. What makes a script interactive?

A) It runs in a terminal window.

B) It prompts the user for input.

C) It executes commands automatically.

D) It is run by multiple users simultaneously.

1. B, 2. B

(Correct)

1. A, 2. B

1. B, 2. A

1. B, 2. C

Explanation

Answer: 1. B) No, because it doesn't interact with the user.

An interactive script requires interaction with the user, such as prompting for input or responding to user actions. This script simply prints "Hello world!" without any user interaction.

Answer: 2. B) It prompts the user for input.

An interactive script engages with the user by prompting for input, displaying messages, or requiring user interaction.

Question 5:

What command is used to filter entries from databases supported by the Name Service Switch (NSS) libraries in Linux?

A) `search`

B) `lookup`

C) `getent`

(Correct)

D) `find`

Explanation

The `getent` command is used to filter entries from databases supported by the Name Service Switch (NSS) libraries in Linux.

Question 6:

How can a user delete an at job with ID 10?

A) deleteat 10

B) atrm 10

(Correct)

C) at -d 10

D) rm at 10

Explanation

The atrm command is used to delete at jobs by specifying their ID.

Question 7:

Which file is used to specify user restrictions for at job scheduling?

A) /etc/at.allow

(Correct)

B) /etc/at.deny

C) /etc/cron.allow

D) /etc/cron.deny

Explanation

The /etc/at.allow file is used to specify which non-root users can schedule at jobs.

Question 8:

What is an alternative to using the at command for one-time task scheduling?

A) cron

B) systemd-run

(Correct)

C) anacron

D) batch

Explanation

systemd-run can be used as an alternative to the at command for one-time task scheduling.

Question 9:

Which systemd option is used to specify the time when a transient timer unit should be activated?

A) --on-time

B) --activate-time

C) --on-calendar

(Correct)

D) --start-time

Explanation

The --on-calendar option is used to specify the time when a

transient timer unit should be activated.

Question 10:

What is the purpose of the /etc/cron.d directory in Linux?

A) To store system crontab files.

(Correct)

B) To specify user restrictions for cron job scheduling.

C) To schedule one-time tasks.

D) To specify the time when a transient timer unit should be activated.

Explanation

The /etc/cron.d directory contains system crontab files.

Question 11:

Which option is used with the crontab command to remove the current crontab?

A) -r

(Correct)

B) -d

C) -l

D) -u

Explanation

The -r option is used with the crontab command to remove the current crontab.

Question 12:

Which environment variable defines the language and character encoding settings for the entire system in Linux?

A) LC_ALL

B) LANG

(Correct)

C) LC_COLLATE

D) LC_TIME

Explanation

The LANG environment variable defines the language and character encoding settings for the entire system in Linux.

Question 13:

What is the purpose of the LC_NUMERIC environment variable in Linux?

A) Sets the time and date format

B) Defines how the system will treat certain sets of characters

C) Sets the numerical format for non-monetary values

(Correct)

D) Sets the standard paper size

Explanation

The LC_NUMERIC environment variable sets the numerical format for non-monetary values, defining the thousand and decimal separators.

Question 14:

Which command can be used to convert text encoding from one format to another in Linux?

A) convert

B) iconv

(Correct)

C) encconv

D) textconv

Explanation

The iconv command is used to convert text encoding from one format to another in Linux.

Question 15:

What is the recommended way to set the local time zone on systemd-based Linux systems?

A) Using the `date` command

B) Editing the /etc/timezone file

C) Using the `timedatectl` command

(Correct)

D) Editing the /etc/localtime file

Explanation

The recommended way to set the local time zone on systemd-based Linux systems is by using the `timedatectl` command.

Question 16:

Which daemon is commonly used to implement NTP in Linux systems?

A) timed

B) ntptime

C) ntpd

(Correct)

D) timesyncd

Explanation

The `ntpd` daemon is commonly used to implement NTP (Network Time Protocol) in Linux systems.

Question 17:

What is the purpose of the `ntpq -p` command?

A) Display system time

B) Print a history of NTP recent polls

(Correct)

C) Check NTP daemon status

D) Configure NTP servers

Explanation

The `ntpq -p` command is used to print a history of NTP (Network Time Protocol) recent polls.

Question 18:

What is the purpose of the 'delaycompress' directive in logrotate configuration?

A) To delay log rotation

B) To delay log compression until the next rotation cycle

(Correct)

C) To disable log compression

D) To prioritize log rotation over compression

Explanation

The 'delaycompress' directive postpones compression of the previous log file to the next rotation cycle, which can be useful when a program continues to write to the previous log file.

Question 19:

Which utility is used to view the kernel ring buffer in Linux?

A) dmesg

(Correct)

B) tail

C) cat

D) grep

Explanation

The dmesg command is used to print the kernel ring buffer, which contains messages generated by the kernel during boot and runtime.

Question 20:

Which directive in rsyslog configuration files is used to define templates for log file names?

A) $FileOwner

B) $FileCreateMode

C) $template

(Correct)

D) $IncludeConfig

Explanation

The $template directive in rsyslog configuration files is used to define templates for log file names, allowing for dynamic formatting based on properties like hostname and timestamp.

Question 21:

What facility and priority level are associated with kernel messages in rsyslog?

A) Facility: kern, Priority: debug

B) Facility: kern, Priority: info

C) Facility: kernel, Priority: emerg

(Correct)

D) Facility: user, Priority: err

Explanation

Kernel messages in rsyslog are associated with the 'kern' facility and can have various priority levels, with 'emerg' being the highest priority level indicating system-wide emergencies.

Question 22:

Which command is used to query the systemd journal in Linux?

A) logger

B) journalctl

(Correct)

C) systemctl

D) dmesg

Explanation

The journalctl command is used to query the systemd journal in Linux, allowing users to view and filter logged messages.

Question 23:

In the context of log rotation, what does the 'notifempty' directive in logrotate configuration indicate?

A) Log files will not be rotated if they are empty

(Correct)

B) Log files will be rotated immediately when empty

C) Log files will be compressed when empty

D) Log files will be deleted if they are not empty

Explanation

The 'notifempty' directive in logrotate configuration specifies that log files will not be rotated if they are empty, ensuring that only non-empty log files are rotated.

Question 24:

What is the purpose of the ~/.forward file in a Unix-like operating system?

A) To configure email aliases for local users

B) To specify the location of the user's mailbox

C) To forward incoming email messages to another email address

(Correct)

D) To configure email filtering rules

Explanation

The ~/.forward file allows users to specify email forwarding rules, redirecting incoming messages to another email address.

Question 25:

Which command can be used to manually send email messages using SMTP commands in a Unix-like operating system?

A) mailq

B) mail

C) nc

(Correct)

D) sendmail

Explanation

The `nc` command (netcat) can be used to manually send SMTP commands to an MTA, allowing users to interact with the email system directly.

Question 26:

Imagine you have changed the values of some variables in ~/.bashrc and want those changes to take effect without a reboot. From your home directory, how could you achieve that in two different ways?

A) Run `source ~/.bashrc` or restart the terminal.

(Correct)

B) Run `exec ~/.bashrc` or logout and log back in.

C) Run `reload ~/.bashrc` or open a new terminal window.

D) Run `update ~/.bashrc` or reset the computer.

Explanation

Running `source ~/.bashrc` reloads the `.bashrc` file in the current shell, applying any changes immediately. Restarting the terminal achieves the same effect by starting a new shell session.

Question 27:

1. John has just started an X Window session on a Linux server. He opens a terminal emulator to carry out some administrative tasks but, surprisingly, the session freezes and he needs to open a text shell. How can he open that tty shell?

A) Press Ctrl + Alt + F1.

B) Use the terminal emulator's menu to switch to a text shell.

C) Use the graphical interface to open a new terminal window.

D) Click on the desktop and choose "Open Terminal."

2. What startup files will get sourced?

A) ~/.bashrc

B) ~/.bash_profile

C) ~/.profile

D) All of the above

1. A, 2. C

1. C, 2. B

1. B, 2. C

1. A, 2. B

(Correct)

Explanation

Answer: 1. A) Press Ctrl + Alt + F1.

Pressing Ctrl + Alt + F1 switches to the first virtual terminal, which typically presents a text-based login prompt.

Answer: 2. B) ~/.bash_profile

When switching to a text-based terminal, the shell typically runs as a login shell, so it sources the `~/.bash_profile` file.

Question 28:

Linda is a user of a Linux server. She kindly asks the

administrator to have a ~/.bash_login file so she can have the time and date printed on the screen when she logs in. Other users like the idea and follow suit. The administrator has a hard time creating the file for all other users on the server so he decides to add a new policy and have ~/.bash_login created for all potential new users. How can the administrator accomplish that task?

A) Edit /etc/bash.bashrc to include commands to create ~/.bash_login for new users.

B) Edit /etc/skel/.bash_login to include the desired commands. **(Correct)**

C) Run `chmod +x ~/.bash_login` to make the file executable for all users.

D) Add a line in /etc/passwd specifying ~/.bash_login as the login shell for new users.

Explanation

The `/etc/skel/` directory contains files and directories that are automatically copied to a new user's home directory when the user is created. By editing `~/.bash_login` in `/etc/skel/`, the administrator ensures that all new users will have this file created with the desired commands when their accounts are set up.

Question 29:

What is the purpose of a variable in a shell environment?

A) To execute commands

B) To store and manipulate data temporarily **(Correct)**

C) To display system information

D) To control user permissions

Explanation

Variables in a shell environment are used to store and manipulate data temporarily, providing a way to reference and reuse information within scripts or commands.

Question 30:

Which command is used to assign a value to a variable in Bash?

A) set

B) define

C) assign

D) export

(Correct)

Explanation

The `export` command is used to assign a value to a variable and make it available to child processes.

Question 31:

What is the syntax for referencing a variable in Bash?

A) $variable_name

(Correct)

B) %variable_name%

C) #variable_name#

D) &variable_name&

Explanation

In Bash, variables are referenced by prefixing the variable name with a dollar sign ($).

Question 32:

Which of the following characters are allowed in variable names in Bash?

A) Spaces

B) Special characters like @ and #

C) Underscores (_) and numbers

(Correct)

D) All of the above

Explanation

Variable names in Bash can contain letters (a-z, A-Z), numbers (0-9), and underscores (_).

Question 33:

What happens if a variable assignment has spaces on either side of the equal sign in Bash?

A) Bash interprets it as a command

(Correct)

B) Bash throws an error

C) The variable is assigned the value within quotes

D) Spaces are ignored

Explanation

If there are spaces on either side of the equal sign in a variable assignment, Bash interprets it as a command rather than a variable assignment.

Question 34:

Which command is used to make a local variable immutable in Bash?

A) readonly

(Correct)

B) immutable

C) lock

D) protect

Explanation

The `readonly` command is used to make a local variable immutable, preventing its value from being changed.

Question 35:

How do you declare an array variable in Bash?

A) Using `array`

B) Using `set`

C) Using `declare -a`

(Correct)

D) Using `define`

Explanation

Arrays are declared in Bash using the `declare -a` command.

Question 36:

What is the purpose of command substitution in shell scripting?

A) To replace shell variables with their values

B) To execute a command and use its output as a value

(Correct)

C) To create aliases for commands

D) To substitute commands with their aliases

Explanation

Command substitution allows the output of a command to replace the command itself in an expression.

Question 37:

How can you execute commands conditionally based on whether the previous command succeeded or failed?

A) Using the `if` statement

B) Using the `test` command

C) Using the `&&` and `||` operators

(Correct)

D) Using the `for` loop

Explanation

The `&&` and `||` operators are used for conditional execution based on the success or failure of the previous command.

Question 38:

Which operator is used for logical OR in shell script conditional statements?

A) `&&`

B) `||`

(Correct)

C) `|`

D) `|&`

Explanation

In shell script conditional statements, `||` is used for logical OR, meaning that the second command is executed only if the first command fails.

Question 39:

What is the purpose of the `test` command in shell scripting?

A) To perform arithmetic operations

B) To compare strings and files

(Correct)

C) To read user input

D) To print formatted output

Explanation

The `test` command is used to evaluate conditional expressions, such as file existence or string comparison, in shell scripting.

Question 40:

The -s option for the read command is useful for entering passwords, as it will not show the content being typed on the screen. How could the read command be used to store the user's input in the variable PASSWORD while hiding the typed content? Options:

A) `read PASSWORD`

B) `read -s PASSWORD`

(Correct)

C) `read -p "Enter Password: " PASSWORD`

D) `read -p PASSWORD`

Explanation

Option B correctly demonstrates the usage of the `-s` option with the `read` command to store user input in the variable PASSWORD while hiding the typed content.

Question 41:

The only purpose of the command whoami is to display the username of the user who called it, so it is mostly used inside scripts to identify the user who is running it. Inside a Bash script, how could the output of the whoami command be stored in the variable named WHO? Options:

A) `WHO=$(whoami)`

(Correct)

B) ` WHO=whoami `

C) ` whoami > WHO `

D) ` $(whoami) > WHO `

Explanation

Option A correctly assigns the output of the ` whoami ` command to the variable WHO using command substitution.

Question 42:

What is the primary version of the X protocol used in modern Linux distributions?

A) X.org version 10

B) X.org version 9

C) X.org version 11

(Correct)

D) X.org version 8

Explanation

X.org version 11, commonly referred to as X11, is the primary version of the X protocol used in modern Linux distributions.

Question 43:

Which component of the X Window System informs the X server about the window location and size on a computer screen?

A) Window manager

B) Display manager

C) X client

(Correct)

D) Desktop environment

Explanation

The X client component of the X Window System informs the X server about the window location and size on a computer screen.

Question 44:

What is the primary responsibility of a display manager in the X Window System?

A) Rendering graphics

B) Managing access to the X server

C) Handling device input

D) Providing a graphical login interface

(Correct)

Explanation

A display manager provides a graphical login interface to the X Window System.

Question 45:

Which component of a desktop environment is responsible for controlling window placement and decorations?

A) File manager

B) Window manager

(Correct)

C) Taskbar

D) Application launcher

Explanation

The window manager controls window placement and decorations, such as adding title bars and control buttons to windows, and managing the switching between open windows.

Question 46:

Which desktop environment is known for its resource efficiency and modular structure?

A) KDE

B) Gnome

C) Xfce

(Correct)

D) LXDE

Explanation

Xfce is known for being aesthetically pleasing while consuming fewer machine resources compared to other desktop environments. Its structure is highly modularized, allowing users to activate and deactivate components according to their needs and preferences.

Question 47:

Which desktop environment is associated with the KDE

Plasma version?

A) Gnome

B) Xfce

C) KDE

(Correct)

D) LXDE

Explanation

KDE Plasma is the latest version of the KDE desktop environment, known for its use of the Qt library and a plethora of original applications.

Question 48:

Which accessibility feature helps inhibit unintended key presses by placing a delay between them?

A) Sticky keys

B) Slow keys

C) Mouse keys

D) Bounce keys

(Correct)

Explanation

Bounce keys help inhibit unintended key presses by placing a delay between them. This feature is particularly helpful for users with hand tremors.

Question 49:

How can users activate the Sticky keys and Slow keys features in Gnome and KDE?

A) Through the mouse gestures

B) By pressing the Shift key five consecutive times

(Correct)

C) By holding down the Alt key

D) By clicking on the screen

Explanation

In Gnome and KDE, users can activate the Sticky keys and Slow keys features by pressing the Shift key five consecutive times.

Question 50:

What feature allows users to control the mouse pointer using the numerical keypad on a keyboard?

A) Sticky keys

B) Slow keys

C) Mouse keys

(Correct)

D) Bounce keys

Explanation

Mouse keys allow users to control the mouse pointer using the numerical keypad on a keyboard. This feature is particularly helpful for users who find it more comfortable to use the keyboard over the mouse.

Question 51:

What command is used to add a new group account in Linux?

A) `addgroup`

B) `groupadd`

(Correct)

C) `newgroup`

D) `creategroup`

Explanation

The `groupadd` command is used to add a new group account in Linux.

Question 52:

Which option of the `groupmod` command is used to change the group name?

A) -n

(Correct)

B) -g

C) -r

D) -m

Explanation

The `-n` option of the `groupmod` command is used to change the group name.

Question 53:

What file specifies the configuration parameters that control the creation of users and groups in Linux?

A) /etc/passwd

B) /etc/group

C) /etc/login.defs

(Correct)

D) /etc/shadow

Explanation

The `/etc/login.defs` file specifies the configuration parameters that control the creation of users and groups in Linux.

Question 54:

Which command is used to change a user's password aging information in Linux?

A) `changepass`

B) `passwd`

C) `userpass`

D) `chage`

(Correct)

Explanation

The `chage` command is used to change a user's password aging information in Linux.

Question 55:

Which command allows users to temporarily join a group if they know the group's password?

A) `join`

B) `addgroup`

C) `newgrp`

(Correct)

D) `userjoin`

Explanation

The `newgrp` command allows users to temporarily join a group if they know the group's password.

Question 56:

Which option is used with the lp command to specify the number of copies to print?

A) -c

B) -n

(Correct)

C) -p

D) -m

Explanation

The -n option is used with the lp command to specify the number of copies to print.

Question 57:

What is the purpose of the lpq command in CUPS?

A) To cancel print jobs

B) To list available printers

C) To view print job queues

(Correct)

D) To enable printer sharing

Explanation

The lpq command is used to view print job queues in CUPS.

Question 58:

Which command is used to cancel a specific print job by its ID?

A) lprm

(Correct)

B) lpstat

C) cancel

D) lp

Explanation

The lprm command is used to cancel a specific print job by its ID.

Question 59:

What is the key difference between TCP and UDP?

A) TCP is connection-oriented, while UDP is connectionless

(Correct)

B) TCP uses port numbers, while UDP uses IP addresses

C) TCP guarantees delivery of packets, while UDP does not

D) TCP is faster than UDP for real-time applications

Explanation

TCP establishes a connection before transmitting data, while UDP does not.

Question 60:

Which protocol is commonly used for sending emails?

A) SMTP

(Correct)

B) DNS

C) HTTP

D) SNMP

Explanation

SMTP (Simple Mail Transfer Protocol) is used for sending emails.

Question 61:

In IPv6, what type of address identifies a set of network interfaces?

A) Unicast

B) Multicast

(Correct)

C) Anycast

D) Broadcast

Explanation

Multicast addresses identify a set of network interfaces.

Question 62:

What is the maximum number of ports available in TCP and UDP?

A) 256

B) 1024

C) 65535

(Correct)

D) 1000000

Explanation

Both TCP and UDP use a 16-bit field for port numbers, allowing for a maximum of 65535 ports.

Question 63:

Which of the following is a characteristic of ICMP?

A) It establishes connections between hosts

B) It provides secure communication

C) It is used for network diagnostics and control

(Correct)

D) It guarantees reliable data delivery

Explanation

ICMP is primarily used for diagnostic and control purposes, such as ping and traceroute.

Question 64:

Which command can be used to view the status of the hostname configuration in Linux?

A) hostctl

B) hostname

C) hostnamectl

(Correct)

D) hoststatus

Explanation

The `hostnamectl` command can be used to view the status of the hostname configuration in Linux.

Question 65:

What is the purpose of the `hosts` line in the `/etc/nsswitch.conf` file?

A) It specifies the DNS server configuration.

B) It defines the loopback interface.

C) It defines the services responsible for providing hostname-to-IP mappings.

(Correct)

D) It specifies the DHCP configuration.

Explanation

The `hosts` line in the `/etc/nsswitch.conf` file specifies the services responsible for providing hostname-to-IP mappings.

Question 66:

What is the purpose of the `ifdown` command in Linux?

A) To bring up a network interface.

B) To configure a network interface.

C) To deactivate a network interface.

(Correct)

D) To view network interface information.

Explanation

The `ifdown` command is used to deactivate a network interface in Linux.

Question 67:

Which command can be used to list network interfaces along with their state and type?

A) ifconfig

B) ip link show

(Correct)

C) nmcli device

D) netstat -i

Explanation

The `ip link show` command lists network interfaces along with their state and type in Linux.

Question 68:

What commands can be used to list the network adapters present in the system? Options:

A) ifconfig, ip addr

(Correct)

B) netstat -i, ip link

C) lspci, lsusb

D) ifup -a, ifdown -a

Explanation

Both `ifconfig` and `ip addr` commands can be used to list the network adapters present in the system.

Question 69:

What is the type of network adapter whose interface name is wlo1? Options:

A) Wired Ethernet

B) Wireless LAN

(Correct)

C) Bluetooth

D) Loopback

Explanation

Interface names starting with "wl" or "wlo" typically indicate wireless LAN adapters.

Question 70:

What role does the file /etc/network/interfaces play during boot time? Options:

A) Manages network settings dynamically

B) Configures DNS settings

C) Specifies routing tables

D) Configures network interfaces

(Correct)

Explanation

The file `/etc/network/interfaces` is used during boot time to configure network interfaces statically or through DHCP.

Question 71:

What entry in /etc/network/interfaces configures interface eno1 to obtain its IP settings with DHCP? Options:

A) `iface eno1 inet static`

B) `iface eno1 inet dhcp`

(Correct)

C) `iface eno1 auto`

D) `iface eno1 dhcp`

Explanation

The entry `iface eno1 inet dhcp` in `/etc/network/interfaces` configures the `eno1` interface to obtain its IP settings using DHCP.

Question 72:

What is the purpose of the `tracepath` command in Linux networking?

A) To trace the route a packet takes to a destination

B) To trace the maximum transmission unit (MTU) along a path

(Correct)

C) To view the routing table

D) To set up arbitrary TCP or UDP connections

Explanation

The `tracepath` command is used to trace the maximum transmission unit (MTU) along a path in Linux networking.

Question 73:

Which command is used to disable or enable an interface in Linux?

A) ip disable

B) ifconfig down

(Correct)

C) route set

D) traceroute

Explanation

The `ifconfig down` command is used to disable an interface in Linux.

Question 74:

What does the `-c` option specify when using the `ping` command in Linux?

A) Number of packets to send

(Correct)

B) IP address to ping

C) Time-to-live (TTL) value

D) Source address to ping from

Explanation

The `-c` option in the `ping` command specifies the number of packets to send.

Question 75:

How does the `traceroute` command determine the route a packet takes to a destination?

A) By sending ICMP echo requests with increasing TTL values

(Correct)

B) By sending UDP packets to port 33434 with increasing TTL values

C) By querying DNS servers along the path

D) By analyzing the routing table on the local system

Explanation

The `traceroute` command determines the route a packet takes to a destination by sending ICMP echo requests with increasing TTL values.

Question 76:

What information does the `netstat` command provide about network connections?

A) Maximum Transmission Unit (MTU) size

B) Round trip time (RTT) for packets

C) Status of current listeners and connections

(Correct)

D) Destination unreachable packet details

Explanation

The `netstat` command provides information about the status of current listeners and connections in Linux networking.

Question 77:

Which command is used to add or remove a route in Linux networking?

A) route modify

B) ifconfig route

C) ip route

(Correct)

D) netstat route

Explanation

The `ip route` command is used to add or remove a route in Linux networking.

Question 78:

What is the purpose of the 'hosts' entry in the /etc/nsswitch.conf file?

A) Configuring DNS servers

B) Configuring local name resolution

(Correct)

C) Configuring network interfaces

D) Configuring firewall rules

Explanation

The 'hosts' entry in /etc/nsswitch.conf specifies how host name resolution should be performed.

Question 79:

Which file is used to configure host resolution via DNS in Linux?

A) /etc/hosts

B) /etc/resolv.conf

(Correct)

C) /etc/nsswitch.conf

D) /etc/network/interfaces

Explanation

The /etc/resolv.conf file is used to configure host resolution via DNS in Linux.

Question 80:

Which command is used to find out who is currently logged in to the system?

A) `last`

B) `whoami`

C) `w`

(Correct)

D) `who`

Explanation

The `w` command shows who is logged in and what they are doing.

Question 81:

Which command is used to set limits on system resources?

A) `ulimit`

(Correct)

B) `limit`

C) `setlimit`

D) `resourcelimit`

Explanation

The `ulimit` command is used to set limits on system resources such as file size, CPU time, and memory usage.

Question 82:

Which configuration file is used to specify user privileges for the `sudo` command?

A) `/etc/passwd`

B) `/etc/sudo.conf`

C) `/etc/sudoers`

(Correct)

D) `/etc/security/limits.conf`

Explanation

The `/etc/sudoers` file is used to specify user privileges for the `sudo` command.

Question 83:

What command is used to list password expiration settings for a user?

A) chage

(Correct)

B) passlist

C) pwexp

D) chsh

Explanation

The chage command lists password expiration settings for a user.

Question 84:

How can you prevent a user from logging into the system temporarily?

A) Delete the user account

B) Change the user's shell to /sbin/nologin

(Correct)

C) Set the user's password to blank

D) Remove the user from the sudoers file

Explanation

Changing the user's shell to /sbin/nologin prevents them from logging in.

Question 85:

Which superdaemon is commonly used to manage network services and start them on demand?

A) init

B) systemd

C) xinetd

(Correct)

D) cron

Explanation

xinetd is a superdaemon commonly used to manage network services and start them on demand.

Question 86:

Which type of port forwarding allows access from the outside to a host on your private network?

A) Local port tunnel

B) Remote port tunnel

(Correct)

C) Dynamic port forwarding

D) X11 tunneling

Explanation

Remote port tunneling (or reverse port forwarding) allows traffic coming to a port on a remote server to be forwarded to the SSH process running on your local host.

Question 87:

What is the minimum recommended key size for DSA keys in OpenSSH?

A) 512 bits

B) 1024 bits

(Correct)

C) 2048 bits

D) 4096 bits

Explanation

The minimum recommended key size for DSA keys in OpenSSH is 1024 bits.

Question 88:

Which command is used to generate SSH key pairs?

A) ssh-agent

B) ssh-keygen

(Correct)

C) ssh-add

D) ssh

Explanation

The `ssh-keygen` command is used to generate SSH key pairs, both for RSA, DSA, ecdsa, and ed25519 algorithms.

Question 89:

What is the purpose of X11 tunneling in SSH?

A) To forward graphical applications from the local host to the remote server

(Correct)

B) To encrypt data transmission between server and client

C) To establish secure remote connections

D) To facilitate file transfers using SCP

Explanation

X11 tunneling (X11 forwarding) allows the X Window System on the remote host to be forwarded to the local machine, enabling the execution of graphical applications remotely.

Question 90:

Which file contains the private keys for the OpenSSH server host?

A) ~/.ssh/id_rsa

B) /etc/ssh/ssh_host_rsa_key

(Correct)

C) ~/.ssh/authorized_keys

D) /etc/ssh/ssh_config

Explanation

The private keys for the OpenSSH server host are stored in files located in the `/etc/ssh/` directory with names like `ssh_host_...._key`.

PRACTICE TEST THREE - LPIC-1 EXAM 102 VERSION: 5.0

90 questions | 2 hours | 90% correct required to pass

The LPIC-1 Exam 102 Version: 5.0 Practice Test is a comprehensive resource designed to prepare you for the LPIC-1 (Linux Professional Institute Certification) Exam 102. It includes practice questions that mimic the format and content of the actual test. Each **Question** comes with a detailed **Explanation** to help you understand the concepts better. This practice test is an excellent tool to harness the power of Linux and achieve LPIC-1 certification.

Question 1:

Which environment variable stores the value of the Bash prompt?

A) PS1

((Correct))

B) PS2

C) PS3

D) PS4

Explanation

The `PS1` environment variable stores the value of the Bash prompt, controlling its appearance.

Question 2:

Observe the variable assignment under the "Command(s)" column and check if the provided resulting variables are "True" or "False":

Command(s)	Local	Global
`debian=mother`	✓	
`ubuntu=deb-based`	✓	
`mint=ubuntu-based; export mint`		✓
`export suse=rpm-based`		✓
`zorin=ubuntu-based`	✓	

A) True

((Correct))

B) False

Explanation

1. debian=mother:

Local: ✓ (The variable debian is assigned the

value mother within the current shell session.)

Global: False (The variable is not exported with export, so it remains local to the current shell.)

2. ubuntu=deb-based:

Local: ✓ (Similar to the previous case, the variable ubuntu is assigned the value deb-based locally.)

Global: False (Not explicitly exported with export.)

3. mint=ubuntu-based; export mint:

Local: False (The mint variable is not declared as a local variable; it is directly exported.)

Global: ✓ (The variable mint is exported with export, making it available globally.)

4. export suse=rpm-based:

Local: False (The variable suse is directly exported; it is not declared as a local variable.)

Global: ✓ (Exporting the variable makes it available globally.)

5. zorin=ubuntu-based:

Local: ✓ (The variable zorin is assigned the value ubuntu-based locally.)

Global: False (Similar to previous cases, it is not exported.)

Understanding variable assignment and scoping is crucial in shell scripting and environment management. By default, variables are local to the shell in which they are defined. However, exporting them with export makes them available to child processes and subsequent shell sessions.

Question 3:

Check if the provided meanings are True or False:

Command	Output	Meaning
`echo $HISTCONTROL`	`ignoreboth`	True
`echo ~`	`/home/carol`	True
`echo $DISPLAY`	`reptilium:0.2`	False
`echo $MAILCHECK`	`60`	True
`echo $HISTFILE`	`/home/carol/.bash_history`	True

A) True

((Correct))

B) False

Explanation

1. echo $HISTCONTROL:

Output: ignoreboth

Meaning: True. $HISTCONTROL is an environment variable in Bash that determines how commands are saved to the history list. The setting ignoreboth tells Bash to ignore commands that start with a space or are duplicates of the previous command.

2. echo ~:

Output: /home/carol

Meaning: True. The tilde ~ is a shortcut for the home directory of a specified user. In this case, it represents the home directory of the user "carol".

3. echo $DISPLAY:

Output: reptilium:0.2

Meaning: False. The output should typically include the display server, screen number, and screen ID. However, the output provided is missing the screen number separator, usually a colon. The correct output should be in the format hostname:displaynumber.screennumber.

4. echo $MAILCHECK:

Output: 60

Meaning: True. $MAILCHECK is an environment variable in Bash that specifies the interval (in seconds) at which Bash checks for mail in the user's mailbox.

5. echo $HISTFILE:

Output: /home/carol/.bash_history

Meaning: True. $HISTFILE is an environment variable in Bash that specifies the location of the history file. In this case, it indicates the history file location for the user "carol".

Understanding the meanings of common environment variables and command outputs is essential for effective shell usage and system administration. These variables control various aspects of the shell's behavior and user environment, influencing command execution and system interaction.

Question 4:

Variables are being set incorrectly under the "Wrong Command" column. Check whether the provided information under "Right Command" is "True" or "False":

Wrong Command	Right Command	Variable Reference	Expected Output
`lizard =chameleon`	`lizard=chameleon`	True	-
`cool lizard=chameleon`	`cool_lizard=chameleon`	True	-
`lizard=cha|me|leon`	`lizard='cha|me|leon'`	True	-
`lizard=/ chameleon /`	`lizard=chameleon`	False	-
`win_path=C:\path\to\dir\`	`win_path="C:\path\to\dir\"`	True	`C:\path\to\dir\`

A) True

((Correct))

B) False

Explanation

1. lizard =chameleon:

Right Command: lizard=chameleon

Variable Reference: True. The correct assignment does not include spaces around the equals sign.

Expected Output: - (No output provided, but the variable is correctly assigned.)

2. cool lizard=chameleon:

Right Command: cool_lizard=chameleon

Variable Reference: True. Variable names cannot contain spaces, so underscores are typically used instead.

Expected Output: - (No output provided, but the variable is correctly assigned.)

3. lizard=cha\|me\|leon:

Right Command: lizard='cha\|me\|leon'

Variable Reference: True. Using single quotes ' ' preserves special characters in the variable value.

Expected Output: - (No output provided, but the variable is correctly assigned.)

4. lizard=/ chameleon /:

Right Command: lizard=chameleon

Variable Reference: False. The provided command contains unnecessary spaces and extra characters that need to be removed.

Expected Output: - (No output provided, but the correct command should only assign chameleon to lizard.)

5. win_path=C:\path\t o\dir\:

Right Command: win_path="C:\path\to\dir\"

Variable Reference: True. Double quotes " " are used to correctly handle spaces and backslashes in the Windows path.

Expected Output: C:\path\to\dir\ (Properly formatted Windows path with backslashes and spaces preserved.)

Understanding how to correctly assign and reference variables in shell scripting is fundamental for ensuring scripts function as intended. Mistakes such as including spaces in variable names or failing to properly escape special characters can lead to errors or unexpected behavior.

Question 5:

Check if the commands provided are related to the purposes:

Purpose	Command
Set the language of the current shell to Spanish UTF-8 (es_ES.UTF-8).	A) `export LANG=es_ES.UTF-8`
Print the name of the current working directory.	B) `pwd`
Reference the environment variable which stores the information about ssh connections.	C) `echo $SSH_CONNECTION`
Set PATH to include /home/carol/scripts as the last directory to search for executables.	D) `export PATH=$PATH:/home/carol/scripts`
Set the value of my_path to PATH.	E) `my_path=$PATH`
Set the value of my_path to that of PATH.	F) `my_path=$PATH`

A) Related

((Correct))

B) Not related

Explanation

A) Set the language of the current shell to Spanish UTF-8 (es_ES.UTF-8):

Command: export LANG=es_ES.UTF-8

Explanation: True. This command sets the environment variable LANG to es_ES.UTF-8, which specifies the language and character encoding for the current shell session.

B) Print the name of the current working directory:

Command: pwd

Explanation: True. The pwd command stands for "print working directory" and outputs the absolute path of the current working directory.

C) Reference the environment variable which stores the information about SSH connections:

Command: echo $SSH_CONNECTION

Explanation: True. $SSH_CONNECTION is an environment variable that stores information about the current SSH connection, including the client's IP address, port, and server's IP address and port.

D) Set PATH to include /home/carol/scripts as the last directory to search for executables:

Command: export PATH=$PATH:/home/carol/scripts

Explanation: True. This command appends /home/carol/scripts to the PATH environment variable, ensuring that executables in that directory are included in the search path.

E) Set the value of my_path to PATH:

Command: my_path=$PATH

Explanation: False. This command assigns the literal string $PATH to the variable my_path, not the contents of the PATH variable itself.

F) Set the value of my_path to that of PATH:

Command: my_path=$PATH

Explanation: True. This command assigns the value of the PATH variable to the variable my_path, effectively copying the contents of PATH into my_path.

Understanding how to set environment variables, reference

them, and use commands to manipulate shell behavior is fundamental for effective shell scripting and system administration. Each command serves a specific purpose related to managing the shell environment or obtaining information about the system's state.

Question 6:

Create a local variable named mammal and assign it the value gnu: Which command accomplishes this task?

A) `mammal=gnu`

((Correct))

B) `set mammal=gnu`

C) `export mammal=gnu`

D) `declare -l mammal=gnu`

Explanation

To create a local variable in Bash, you simply assign a value to it without using any special command. Option A achieves this by assigning the value "gnu" to the variable mammal.

Question 7:

Using variable substitution, create another local variable named var_sub with the appropriate value so that when referenced via echo $var_sub we obtain: The value of mammal is gnu: Which command correctly achieves this?

A) `var_sub="The value of mammal is gnu"`

B) `var_sub="The value of mammal is ${gnu}"`

C) `var_sub="The value of mammal is ${mammal}"`

((Correct))

D) `var_sub="The value of mammal is $mammal"`

Explanation

Option C uses variable substitution to include the value of the variable mammal within the string assigned to var_sub.

Question 8:

Turn mammal into an environment variable: What command is used to turn a local variable into an environment variable?

A) `export mammal`

((Correct))

B) `setenv mammal`

C) `env mammal`

D) `declare -x mammal`

Explanation

The `export` command is used to turn a local variable into an environment variable in Bash. Option A achieves this by exporting the variable mammal.

Question 9:

What Bash operator should be between the commands `apt-get dist-upgrade` and `systemctl reboot` if the root user wants to execute `systemctl reboot` only if `apt-get dist-upgrade` finished successfully. Options:

A) `|`

B) `>`

C) ` && `

((**Correct**))

D) ` || `

Explanation

Option C correctly indicates the Bash operator ` && `, which ensures that the command following it (`systemctl reboot`) is executed only if the command preceding it (`apt-get dist-upgrade`) exits with a success status.

Question 10:

After trying to run a newly created Bash script, a user receives the following error message: `bash: ./script.sh: Permission denied`. Considering that the file ./script.sh was created by the same user, what would be the probable cause of this error? Options:

A) The file is not found

B) The script lacks execute permissions

((**Correct**))

C) The script is corrupted

D) The user has insufficient disk space

Explanation

Option B is correct. The error "Permission denied" typically occurs when the script lacks execute permissions for the user trying to run it.

Question 11:

Suppose a script file named do.sh is executable and the symbolic link named undo.sh points to it. From within the script, how could you identify if the calling filename was do.sh or undo.sh? Options:

A) `basename "$0"`

((Correct))

B) `echo $0`

C) `pwd`

D) `readlink -f "$0"`

Explanation

Option A correctly identifies the filename that was used to call the script, regardless of whether it was do.sh or undo.sh.

Question 12:

In a system with a properly configured email service, the command mail -s "Maintenance Error" root <<<"Scheduled task error" sends the notice email message to the root user. Such a command could be used in unattended tasks, like cronjobs, to inform the system administrator about an unexpected issue. Write an if construct that will execute the aforementioned mail command if the exit status of the previous command — whatever it was — is unsuccessful. Options:

A) `if [ $? -eq 0 ]; then mail -s "Maintenance Error" root <<<"Scheduled task error"; fi`

B) `if [ $? -eq 1 ]; then mail -s "Maintenance Error" root <<<"Scheduled task error"; fi`

C) `if [$? -ne 0]; then mail -s "Maintenance Error" root

<<<"Scheduled task error"; fi `

((**Correct**))

D) `if [ $? -ne 1 ]; then mail -s "Maintenance Error" root <<<"Scheduled task error"; fi `

Explanation

Option C correctly constructs an if statement that checks if the exit status of the previous command (` $?`) is not equal to 0, indicating an unsuccessful execution, and then executes the mail command to notify the root user about the error.

Question 13:

Which of the following commands is used to test if a directory exists in a Bash script?

A) `test -d /path/to/directory`

((**Correct**))

B) `[-d /path/to/directory]`

C) `test -f /path/to/directory`

D) `[ -f /path/to/directory]`

Explanation

The `-d` option in the `test` command or its equivalent `[ ]` syntax is used to test if a directory exists.

Question 14:

What does the following test evaluate in a Bash script: `[ "$VAR" = "value" ]`?

A) Checks if ` $VAR` is not equal to "value".

B) Checks if `$VAR` is equal to "value".

((Correct))

C) Checks if `$VAR` exists.

D) Checks if `$VAR` is empty.

Explanation

This test checks if the value of the variable `$VAR` is equal to "value".

Question 15:

Which loop construct in Bash executes a set of commands until a test command terminates with status 0 (success)?

A) `for`

B) `until`

((Correct))

C) `while`

D) `if`

Explanation

The `until` loop executes a set of commands until a test command terminates with status 0 (success).

Question 16:

In an X Window System, what does the term "DISPLAY" environment variable specify?

A) Screen resolution

B) X server version

C) Display name and details

((**Correct**))

D) Window manager configuration

Explanation

The "DISPLAY" environment variable specifies the display name and details of the running X server.

Question 17:

Which command is used to display information about a running X server instance in Linux?

A) xinfo

B) xstatus

C) xdisplay

D) xdpyinfo

((**Correct**))

Explanation

The "xdpyinfo" command is used to display information about a running X server instance in Linux.

Question 18:

What is the purpose of the xorg.conf file in X server configuration?

A) To store display manager settings

B) To configure keyboard and mouse input

C) To define the layout of windows

D) To specify monitor and video card settings

((Correct))

Explanation

The xorg.conf file is used to specify monitor and video card settings in X server configuration.

Question 19:

Which organization maintains a large body of specifications for desktop interoperability in Linux-based operating systems?

A) GNOME Foundation

B) Linux Foundation

C) freedesktop.org

((Correct))

D) X.org Foundation

Explanation

freedesktop.org maintains a large body of specifications for desktop interoperability in Linux-based operating systems, including specifications for directories locations, desktop entries, application autostart, drag and drop, trash can, and icon themes.

Question 20:

Which protocol is used by the X Window System to communicate with remote displays for remote desktop sessions?

A) SSH

B) VNC

C) RDP

D) XDMCP

((**Correct**))

Explanation

The X Window System uses the X Display Manager Control Protocol (XDMCP) to communicate with remote displays for remote desktop sessions.

Question 21:

Which remote desktop protocol is mainly used to access the desktop of a Microsoft Windows operating system?

A) VNC

B) RDP

((**Correct**))

C) XDMCP

D) Spice

Explanation

The Remote Desktop Protocol (RDP) is mainly used to remotely access the desktop of a Microsoft Windows operating system through the TCP 3389 network port.

Question 22:

Which screen reader is commonly installed by default in most

Linux distributions?

A) Orca

((Correct))

B) JAWS

C) NVDA

D) VoiceOver

Explanation

Orca is commonly installed by default in most Linux distributions as a screen reader.

Question 23:

What feature in Gnome provides options to make windows and buttons easier to see by drawing them in sharper colors?

A) High Contrast

((Correct))

B) Large Text

C) Cursor Size

D) Zoom

Explanation

The High Contrast feature in Gnome provides options to make windows and buttons easier to see by drawing them in sharper colors.

Question 24:

Which tool in KDE provides features similar to Gnome's High

Contrast, Large Text, and Cursor Size options?

A) KMagnifier

B) KMouseTool

C) Universal Access

D) System Settings

((Correct))

Explanation

System Settings in KDE provides features similar to Gnome's High Contrast, Large Text, and Cursor Size options for accessibility settings.

Question 25:

Check if the commands provided are related to the purposes:

Command: Purpose

usermod -L: Lock user account

passwd -u: Unlock user account

chage -E: Set password aging information

groupdel: Delete a group

useradd -s: Add a new user account with a home directory

groupadd -g: Add a new group with a specific GID

userdel -r: Delete a user account and its home directory

usermod -l: Change user login name

groupmod -n: Rename a group

useradd -m: Add a new user account with a home directory

A) Related

((**Correct**))

B) Not related

Explanation

Each command has a specific purpose related to managing user accounts and groups in Linux.

Question 26:

Check if the commands provided are related to the purposes:

Command: Purpose

passwd -n: Set the minimum number of days between password changes

passwd -x: Set the maximum number of days a password is valid

passwd -w: Set the number of days warning users receive before password expiration

passwd -i: Set the inactive period after password expiration

passwd -S: Display password status information

A) Related

((**Correct**))

B) Not related

Explanation

passwd -n: Set the minimum number of days between password changes.

Explanation: True. The -n option with passwd allows setting the minimum number of days required before a user can change their password.

passwd -x: Set the maximum number of days a password is valid.

Explanation: True. The -x option with passwd sets the maximum number of days a password remains valid before it expires.

passwd -w: Set the number of days warning users receive before password expiration.

Explanation: True. The -w option with passwd configures the number of days in advance that users are warned before their password expires.

passwd -i: Set the inactive period after password expiration.

Explanation: True. The -i option with passwd sets the inactive period after the expiration of a password.

passwd -S: Display password status information.

Explanation: True. The -S option with passwd displays password status information, including password aging information and other relevant details.

Understanding the various options available with the passwd command is crucial for managing user account passwords and enforcing password policies in a Linux system.

These options allow administrators to configure password-related parameters, such as expiration periods, warning periods, and inactivity periods, to ensure system security and compliance with organizational policies.

Question 27:

Check if the commands provided are related to the purposes:

Command	Purpose
`usermod -L`	Locks a user account by placing a ! character in front of the encrypted password in the /etc/shadow file, effectively preventing the user from logging in.
`passwd -u`	Unlocks a previously locked user account by removing the ! character from the encrypted password in the /etc/shadow file.
`chage -E`	Sets the expiration date for an account. This command is often used to define a specific end date for a user account's validity.
`groupdel`	Deletes a specified group from the system, removing it from the /etc/group file and disassociating it from any users who were members of the group.
`useradd -s`	Adds a new user account with the specified login shell, defining the shell that the user will interact with upon logging in.
`groupadd -g`	Adds a new group with a specific GID (Group ID), ensuring that the group is created with a particular numerical identifier.
`userdel -r`	Deletes a user account and removes associated files, including the user's home directory and any files stored within it.
`usermod -l`	Modifies the login name of an existing user account, changing the username that the user must provide to log in.
`groupmod -n`	Renames an existing group, allowing administrators to change the name of a group without altering its GID or associated user memberships.
`useradd -m`	Adds a new user account along with a home directory, creating the specified user's home directory if it does not already exist.

A) Related

((Correct))

B) Not related

Explanation

usermod -L: Locks a user account by placing a ! character in front of the encrypted password in the /etc/shadow file, effectively preventing the user from logging in.

Explanation: True. The -L option with usermod is used to lock a user account by adding a ! character in front of the encrypted password in the /etc/shadow file, thereby preventing login.

passwd -u: Unlocks a previously locked user account by removing the ! character from the encrypted password in the /etc/shadow file.

Explanation: True. The -u option with passwd is used to unlock a previously locked user account by removing the ! character from the encrypted password in the /etc/shadow file, allowing login.

chage -E: Sets the expiration date for an account. This command is often used to define a specific end date for a user account's validity.

Explanation: True. The -E option with chage sets the expiration date for an account, allowing administrators to define a specific end date for the user account's validity.

groupdel: Deletes a specified group from the system, removing it from the /etc/group file and disassociating it from any users who were members of the group.

Explanation: True. The groupdel command deletes a specified group from the system, removing it from the /etc/group file and disassociating it from any users who were members of the group.

useradd -s: Adds a new user account with the specified login shell, defining the shell that the user will interact with upon logging in.

Explanation: True. The -s option with useradd is used to specify the login shell for a new user account, defining the shell that the user will interact with upon logging in.

groupadd -g: Adds a new group with a specific GID (Group ID), ensuring that the group is created with a particular numerical identifier.

Explanation: True. The -g option with groupadd specifies the GID (Group ID) for the new group, ensuring that it is created with the specified numerical identifier.

userdel -r: Deletes a user account and removes associated files, including the user's home directory and any files stored within it.

Explanation: True. The -r option with userdel removes the user's home directory and its contents along with deleting the user account.

usermod -l: Modifies the login name of an existing user account, changing the username that the user must provide to log in.

Explanation: True. The -l option with usermod is used to modify the login name of an existing user account, effectively changing the username that the user must provide to log in.

groupmod -n: Renames an existing group, allowing administrators to change the name of a group without altering its GID or associated user memberships.

Explanation: True. The -n option with groupmod allows

administrators to rename an existing group without altering its GID or associated user memberships.

useradd -m: Adds a new user account along with a home directory, creating the specified user's home directory if it does not already exist.

Explanation: True. The -m option with useradd ensures that a home directory is created for the new user account, including any necessary files and directories.

Understanding the purposes and options of commands related to user and group management is crucial for system administrators to effectively manage user accounts and permissions on Linux systems. Each command serves a specific function in user and group administration, facilitating tasks such as account creation, modification, deletion, and password management.

Question 28:

Using the groupadd command, create the administrators and developers groups. Assume you are working as root. Options:

A) groupadd administrators && groupadd developers

((Correct))

B) groupadd -G administrators,developers

C) groupadd -n administrators && groupadd -n developers

D) groupadd -g administrators && groupadd -g developers

Explanation

Option A correctly demonstrates the use of the groupadd command to create two new groups named administrators and developers.

Question 29:

Assuming you have created the administrators and developers groups, run the following command: `useradd -G administrators,developers kevin`. What operations does this command perform? Assume that CREATE_HOME and USERGROUPS_ENAB in /etc/login.defs are set to yes.

Options:

A) It creates a new user account named kevin and assigns it to both the administrators and developers groups, with a home directory created for the user.

((Correct))

B) It modifies the kevin user account, adding it to the administrators and developers groups, without creating a home directory.

C) It creates a new user account named kevin without adding it to any groups.

D) It adds the administrators and developers groups as secondary groups for the existing kevin user account.

Explanation

Option A accurately describes the command's function, which adds the user kevin to both the administrators and developers groups and creates a home directory for the user.

Question 30:

Create a new group named designers, rename it to web-designers, and add this new group to the secondary groups of the kevin user account. Identify all the groups kevin belongs to and their IDs. Options:

A) groups kevin

B) groupmod -n web-designers designers && usermod -aG designers,web-designers kevin

C) groupadd designers && groupmod -n web-designers designers && usermod -aG web-designers kevin

D) groupadd designers && groupmod -n web-designers designers && usermod -aG designers,web-designers kevin

((Correct))

Explanation

Option D correctly outlines the necessary commands to create the designers group, rename it to web-designers, and add it to the secondary groups of the user kevin.

Question 31:

Check if the corresponding time specifications mentioned for each of the mentioned crontab shortcuts "True" or "False":

1. `@hourly`: This runs once an hour, at the beginning of the hour.

Time specification: `0 * * * *`

2. `@daily`: This runs once a day, at midnight (00:00).

Time specification: `0 0 * * *`

3. `@weekly`: This runs once a week, on Sunday at midnight (00:00).

Time specification: `0 0 * * 0`

4. `@monthly`: This runs once a month, on the first day of the

month at midnight (00:00).

Time specification: `0 0 1 * *`

5. `@annually`: This runs once a year, on January 1st at midnight (00:00).

Time specification: `0 0 1 1 *`

A) True

((Correct))

B) False

Explanation

Let's break down the crontab shortcuts and their corresponding time specifications:

@hourly:

Time Specification: 0 * * * *

Explanation: This runs the job every hour at the zeroth minute (i.e., at the start of each hour).

@daily:

Time Specification: 0 0 * * *

Explanation: This runs the job once a day at midnight (00:00).

@weekly:

Time Specification: 0 0 * * 0

Explanation: This runs the job once a week on Sunday (since Sunday is represented by 0 in the fifth field).

@monthly:

Time Specification: 0 0 1 * *

Explanation: This runs the job once a month on the first day of the month.

@annually (also known as @yearly):

Time Specification: 0 0 1 1 *

Explanation: This runs the job once a year on January 1st.

Remember that the first five columns represent the minutes, hours, days of the month, months, and days of the week, respectively. The asterisks (*) indicate that the job should run for all possible values in that field.

Question 32:

How can a local variable be turned into an environment variable in Bash?

A) Using the declare command

B) Using the export command

((Correct))

C) Using the set command

D) Using the env command

Explanation

The `export` command is used to make a local variable an environment variable in Bash.

Question 33:

Which command is used to unset a variable in Bash?

A) delete

B) remove

C) unset

((Correct))

D) clear

Explanation

The `unset` command is used to unset or remove a variable in Bash.

Question 34:

What is the purpose of the `env` command in Bash?

A) To list all environment variables

B) To set environment variables

C) To execute a program in a modified environment

D) All of the above

((Correct))

Explanation

The `env` command can be used to list all environment variables, set environment variables, and execute a program in a modified environment.

Question 35:

Which environment variable stores the absolute path of the current user's home directory?

A) USER

B) HOME

((Correct))

C) PATH

D) SHELL

Explanation

The `HOME` environment variable stores the absolute path of the current user's home directory.

Question 36:

What does the `HISTCONTROL` environment variable control in Bash?

A) The number of commands stored in memory

B) The frequency of checking for new mail

C) Which commands are saved into the history file

((Correct))

D) The locale of the system

Explanation

The `HISTCONTROL` environment variable controls which commands are saved into the history file in Bash.

Question 37:

Check if the corresponding time specifications (the longer normalized form) for each of the mentioned OnCalendar shortcuts are "True" or "False":

1. `hourly`: *-*-* *:00/1:00

This runs once an hour, at the beginning of the hour.

2. `daily`: *-*-* 00:00:00

This runs once a day, at midnight (00:00).

3. `weekly`: Mon *-*-* 00:00:00

This runs once a week, on Monday at midnight (00:00).

4. `monthly`: *-01 *-* 00:00:00

This runs once a month, on the first day of the month at midnight (00:00).

5. `yearly`: Jan 1 *-* 00:00:00

This runs once a year, on January 1st at midnight (00:00).

A) True

((Correct))

B) False

Explanation

The longer normalized form refers to the expanded version of the OnCalendar expressions, which provides a more detailed breakdown of the timing. It includes the specific values for each component of the schedule: year, month, day, hour, minute, and second.

Here's the breakdown of the longer normalized form:

Year: Specified as four digits (e.g., 2024).

Month: Specified as two digits (01 for January, 02 for February, etc.).

Day: Specified as two digits (01 for the first day, 02 for the second day, etc.).

Hour: Specified as two digits in 24-hour format (00 for midnight, 01 for 1:00 AM, etc.).

Minute: Specified as two digits (00 through 59).

Second: Specified as two digits (00 through 59).

For example:

`*-*-* *:00/1:00` translates to every hour (`*` for every possible value in year, month, and day) at the beginning of the hour (`*:00`), with a step size of 1 hour (`/1:00`).

`*-*-* 00:00:00` translates to every day (`*` for every possible value in year, month, and day) at midnight (`00:00:00`).

`Mon *-*-* 00:00:00` translates to every Monday (`Mon`) at midnight (`00:00:00`).

`*-01 *-* 00:00:00` translates to every month on the first day (`*-01`) at midnight (`00:00:00`).

`Jan 1 *-* 00:00:00` translates to every January 1st (`Jan 1`) at midnight (`00:00:00`).

Question 38:

Check if the meaning of the following time specifications

found in a crontab file are "True" or "False":

1. `30 13 * * 1-5`: This specification means the following:

The command will run at 1:30 PM (13:30) every day from Monday to Friday (Monday through Friday).

2. `00 09-18 * * *`: This specification means the following:

The command will run every hour (00 minutes past the hour) from 9:00 AM to 6:00 PM (18:00), every day of the month, every month, and every day of the week.

3. `30 08 1 1 *`: This specification means the following:

The command will run at 8:30 AM (08:30) on the 1st day of January (the beginning of the year).

4. `0,20,40 11 * * Sun`: This specification means the following:

The command will run at 11:00 AM (11:00), 11:20 AM (11:20), and 11:40 AM (11:40) on Sundays.

5. `*/20 * * * *`: This specification means the following:

The command will run every 20 minutes (at 00, 20, and 40 minutes past the hour), every hour, every day of the month, every month, and every day of the week.

A) True

((Correct))

B) False

Explanation

Let's break down each of the time specifications found in a crontab file:

1. `30 13 * * 1-5`: This specification means the following:

The command will run at 1:30 PM (13:30) every day from Monday to Friday (Monday through Friday).

2. `00 09-18 * * *`: This specification means the following:

The command will run every hour (00 minutes past the hour) from 9:00 AM to 6:00 PM (18:00), every day of the month, every month, and every day of the week.

3. `30 08 1 1 *`: This specification means the following:

The command will run at 8:30 AM (08:30) on the 1st day of January (the beginning of the year).

4. `0,20,40 11 * * Sun`: This specification means the following:

The command will run at 11:00 AM (11:00), 11:20 AM (11:20), and 11:40 AM (11:40) on Sundays.

5. `*/20 * * * *`: This specification means the following:

The command will run every 20 minutes (at 00, 20, and 40 minutes past the hour), every hour, every day of the month, every month, and every day of the week.

Question 39:

Check if the meaning of the following time specifications used in the OnCalendar option of a timer file are "True" or "False":

1. `` `*-*-* 08:30:00` ``: This specification means the following:

The timer will trigger every day at 08:30:00 (8:30 AM) regardless of the year, month, or day of the month.

2. `` `Sat,Sun *-*-* 05:00:00` ``: This specification means the following:

The timer will trigger every Saturday and Sunday at 05:00:00 (5:00 AM) regardless of the year, month, or day of the month.

3. `` `*-*-01 13:15,30,45:00` ``: This specification means the following:

The timer will trigger on the first day of every month at 13:15:00, 13:30:00, and 13:45:00 (1:15 PM, 1:30 PM, and 1:45 PM) regardless of the year.

4. `` `Fri *-09..12-* 16:20:00` ``: This specification means the following:

The timer will trigger every Friday between September and December at 16:20:00 (4:20 PM) regardless of the year.

5. `` `Mon,Tue *-*-1,15 08:30:00` ``: This specification means the following:

The timer will trigger on Mondays and Tuesdays on the 1st and 15th day of every month at 08:30:00 (8:30 AM) regardless of the year.

6. `` `*-*-* *:00/05:00` ``: This specification means the following:

The timer will trigger every 5 minutes, starting at the

beginning of the hour, regardless of the year, month, day of the month, or day of the week.

A) True

((**Correct**))

B) False

Explanation

Let's break down each of the time specifications used in the OnCalendar option of a timer file:

1. `` `*-*-* 08:30:00` ``: This specification means the following:

The timer will trigger every day at 08:30:00 (8:30 AM) regardless of the year, month, or day of the month.

2. `` `Sat,Sun *-*-* 05:00:00` ``: This specification means the following:

The timer will trigger every Saturday and Sunday at 05:00:00 (5:00 AM) regardless of the year, month, or day of the month.

3. `` `*-*-01 13:15,30,45:00` ``: This specification means the following:

The timer will trigger on the first day of every month at 13:15:00, 13:30:00, and 13:45:00 (1:15 PM, 1:30 PM, and 1:45 PM) regardless of the year.

4. `` `Fri *-09..12-* 16:20:00` ``: This specification means the following:

The timer will trigger every Friday between September and December at 16:20:00 (4:20 PM) regardless of the year.

5. `**Mon,Tue \*-\*-1,15 08:30:00**`: This specification means the following:

The timer will trigger on Mondays and Tuesdays on the 1st and 15th day of every month at 08:30:00 (8:30 AM) regardless of the year.

6. `**\*-\*-\* \*:00/05:00**`: This specification means the following:

The timer will trigger every 5 minutes, starting at the beginning of the hour, regardless of the year, month, day of the month, or day of the week.

Question 40:

Assuming that you are authorized to schedule jobs with cron as an ordinary user, what command would you use to create your own crontab file? Options:

A) crontab -e

((Correct))

B) crontab -l

C) cron -u

D) cron -f

Explanation

Option A (`crontab -e`) allows an ordinary user to create or edit their own crontab file.

Question 41:

Create a simple scheduled job that executes the date command every Friday at 01:00 PM. Where can you see the output of this job? Options:

A) /var/log/cron

B) /var/log/syslog

C) /var/spool/cron/crontabs

((Correct))

D) /var/log/messages

Explanation

Option C is correct because the crontab files are stored in the /var/spool/cron/crontabs directory.

Question 42:

What is the default time zone used by cloud services to mitigate occasional inconsistencies between local time and time at clients or other servers?

A) GMT+0

((Correct))

B) GMT-5

C) GMT+3

D) GMT+8

Explanation

Cloud services commonly use the UTC (GMT+0) time zone to mitigate occasional inconsistencies between local time and time at clients or other servers.

Question 43:

Which command shows more detailed information about the system time and date, including the time zone, in Linux distributions using systemd?

A) date

B) timedatectl

((Correct))

C) tzselect

D) locale

Explanation

The timedatectl command shows more detailed information about the system time and date, including the time zone, in Linux distributions using systemd.

Question 44:

What is the purpose of setting the hardware clock to UTC in a Linux system?

A) To synchronize with remote servers

B) To optimize system performance

C) To mitigate inconsistencies between local time and time at clients or other servers

((Correct))

D) To improve security measures

Explanation

Setting the hardware clock to UTC helps mitigate occasional inconsistencies between local time and time at clients or other servers in a Linux system.

Question 45:

Which file contains configuration information about how a Linux system synchronizes with network time?

A) /etc/timezone

B) /etc/ntp.conf

((Correct))

C) /etc/localtime

D) /etc/chrony.conf

Explanation

The `/etc/ntp.conf` file contains configuration information about how a Linux system synchronizes with network time using NTP (Network Time Protocol).

Question 46:

Which command is used to perform a manual one-time NTP step update?

A) ntpupdate

B) ntpsync

C) ntpstep

D) ntpdate

((Correct))

Explanation

The `ntpdate` command is used to perform a manual one-time NTP step update in Linux.

Question 47:

What is the primary purpose of the NTP Pool project?

A) To provide NTP servers for commercial use

B) To distribute network load among many machines

((Correct))

C) To create a hierarchical structure for NTP synchronization

D) To provide NTP servers for government agencies

Explanation

The primary purpose of the NTP Pool project is to distribute network load among many machines by providing a pool of NTP servers.

Question 48:

Check if the provided utilities/commands can be used in the following scenarios:

Purpose and log file: Utility

Read /var/log/syslog.7.gz: *zcat*

Read /var/log/syslog: *cat*

Filter for the word renewal in /var/log/syslog: *grep*

Read /var/log/faillog: *last*

Read /var/log/syslog dynamically: *tail*

A) Yes

((Correct))

B) No

Explanation

Read /var/log/syslog.7.gz: *zcat*

Explanation: True. zcat is used to read compressed files with the .gz extension. It can read syslog.7.gz directly and display its content without needing to decompress the file explicitly.

Read /var/log/syslog: *cat*

Explanation: True. cat is a versatile command that can concatenate and display the content of files. It can be used to read syslog directly.

Filter for the word renewal in /var/log/syslog: *grep*

Explanation: True. grep is a powerful tool for searching and filtering text. It can be used to filter lines containing specific words or patterns, such as "renewal" in syslog.

Read /var/log/faillog: *last*

Explanation: False. last command is typically used to display the login history of users, not to read log files like faillog. To read faillog, you would typically use faillog command.

Read /var/log/syslog dynamically: *tail*

Explanation: True. tail command is commonly used to display the last few lines of a file, making it suitable for dynamically reading log files such as syslog to monitor ongoing activity or errors.

Understanding the functionalities and use cases of various utilities and commands is crucial for system administrators and users working with Linux systems. Each command serves a specific purpose, and knowing which command to use in a given scenario enhances efficiency and productivity in managing and troubleshooting systems.

Question 49:

Rearrange the following log entries in such a way that they represent a valid log message with the proper structure:

∘ *debian-server*

∘ *sshd*

∘ *[515]:*

∘ *Sep 13 21:47:56*

∘ *Server listening on 0.0.0.0 port 22*

Options:

A) *debian-server Sep 13 21:47:56 sshd[515]: Server listening on 0.0.0.0 port 22*

B) *Sep 13 21:47:56 debian-server sshd[515]: Server listening on 0.0.0.0 port 22*

C) *Sep 13 21:47:56 sshd[515]: debian-server Server listening on 0.0.0.0 port 22*

D) *sshd[515]: debian-server Sep 13 21:47:56 Server listening on 0.0.0.0 port 22*

A) *debian-server Sep 13 21:47:56 sshd[515]: Server listening on 0.0.0.0 port 22*

B) *Sep 13 21:47:56 debian-server sshd[515]: Server listening on 0.0.0.0 port 22*

((Correct))

C) *Sep 13 21:47:56 sshd[515]: debian-server Server listening on 0.0.0.0 port 22*

D) *sshd[515]: debian-server Sep 13 21:47:56 Server listening on 0.0.0.0 port 22*

Explanation

The correct order for a log message is: Timestamp, Hostname, Program name, Process ID, Message.

Question 50:

Can the provided rules, when added to /etc/rsyslog.conf, accomplish the specified tasks?

Task: Rule

1. Send all messages from the mail facility and a priority/ severity of crit (and above) to /var/log/mail.crit:

Rule: *mail.*;mail.crit /var/log/mail.crit*

2. Send all messages from the mail facility with priorities of alert and emergency to /var/log/mail.urgent:

Rule: *mail.alert,mail.emerg /var/log/mail.urgent*

3. Except for those coming from the cron and ntp facilities, send all messages — irrespective of their facility and priority — to /var/log/allmessages:

Rule: *!cron, !ntp /var/log/allmessages*

4. With all required settings properly configured first, send all messages from the mail facility to a remote host whose IP address is 192.168.1.88 using TCP and specifying the default port:

Rule: *mail.* @@192.168.1.88:514*

5. Irrespective of their facility, send all messages with the warning priority (only with the warning priority) to /var/log/warnings preventing excessive writing to the disk:

Rule: **.warning /var/log/warnings*

A) Yes

((**Correct**))

B) No

Explanation

1. Send all messages from the mail facility and a priority/severity of crit (and above) to /var/log/mail.crit:

Rule: *mail.*;mail.crit /var/log/mail.crit*

Explanation: True. This rule sends all messages from the mail facility (mail.*) with a priority of crit and higher to /var/log/mail.crit.

2. Send all messages from the mail facility with priorities of alert and emergency to /var/log/mail.urgent:

Rule: *mail.alert,mail.emerg /var/log/mail.urgent*

Explanation: True. This rule sends messages from the mail facility with priorities of alert and emergency to /var/log/

mail.urgent.

3. Except for those coming from the cron and ntp facilities, send all messages — irrespective of their facility and priority — to /var/log/allmessages:

Rule: *!cron, !ntp /var/log/allmessages*

Explanation: True. This rule excludes messages from the cron and ntp facilities and sends all other messages to /var/log/allmessages.

4. With all required settings properly configured first, send all messages from the mail facility to a remote host whose IP address is 192.168.1.88 using TCP and specifying the default port:

Rule: *mail.* @@192.168.1.88:514*

Explanation: True. This rule sends all messages from the mail facility (mail.*) to the remote host 192.168.1.88 using TCP and the default port 514.

5. Irrespective of their facility, send all messages with the warning priority (only with the warning priority) to /var/log/warnings preventing excessive writing to the disk:

Rule: **.warning /var/log/warnings*

Explanation: True. This rule sends all messages with the priority of warning to /var/log/warnings, regardless of their facility.

Understanding how to configure rules in the /etc/rsyslog.conf file is essential for managing and routing log messages in a Linux system effectively. Rsyslog provides powerful capabilities for filtering and directing log messages based on various criteria, including facility, priority, and destination. Properly configured rules help ensure that relevant log messages are captured, processed, and stored or forwarded as needed for monitoring, analysis, and troubleshooting purposes.

Question 51:

Check whether the explanations given for the following passages from /etc/logrotate.d/samba are correct or not.

Passage: Explanation

weekly: Specifies the frequency of log rotation as weekly.

missingok: Ignores errors if the log file is missing.

rotate 7: Keeps only 7 rotated log files.

postrotate: Executes the commands in the following block after log rotation.

endscript: Marks the end of the script section in the log rotation configuration.

compress: Enables compression of rotated log files.

delaycompress: Delays compression until the next rotation cycle.

notifempty: Does not rotate empty log files.

A) (Correct)

((Correct))

B) Not correct

Explanation

weekly: Specifies the frequency of log rotation as weekly.

Explanation: True. This parameter instructs logrotate to rotate the logs weekly, meaning it will perform log rotation once every week.

missingok: Ignores errors if the log file is missing.

Explanation: True. This parameter tells logrotate not to issue an error if the log file specified does not exist. It continues with the rotation process regardless.

rotate 7: Keeps only 7 rotated log files.

Explanation: False. This parameter specifies that logrotate keeps only 7 rotated log files, rotating out older files as new ones are created.

postrotate: Executes the commands in the following block after log rotation.

Explanation: True. This keyword indicates the beginning of the post-rotation script block. Commands specified within this block will be executed after log rotation completes.

endscript: Marks the end of the script section in the log rotation configuration.

Explanation: True. This keyword marks the end of the script block, demarcating the end of the commands to be executed after log rotation.

compress: Enables compression of rotated log files.

Explanation: True. This parameter directs logrotate to compress rotated log files after they have been rotated, saving disk space.

delaycompress: Delays compression until the next rotation cycle.

Explanation: True. This parameter instructs logrotate to delay the compression of log files until the next rotation cycle. This ensures that the currently rotated file is not compressed immediately after rotation, allowing for potential post-rotation processing.

notifempty: Does not rotate empty log files.

Explanation: True. This parameter specifies that logrotate should not rotate empty log files. It ensures that only log files with content are rotated, preventing unnecessary rotation of empty files.

Understanding the parameters used in log rotation configuration files like /etc/logrotate.d/samba is crucial for effectively managing log files in a Linux system. These parameters control various aspects of log rotation behavior, including frequency, compression, error handling, and post-rotation actions. Properly configured log rotation settings help maintain log file integrity, manage disk space efficiently, and facilitate log analysis and troubleshooting.

Question 52:

In the section "Templates and Filter Conditions," we explored expression-based filters as a filter condition. Another type of filter unique to rsyslogd is property-based filters. Translate the expression-based filter into a property-based filter:

Expression-Based Filter   **Property-Based Filter**

if $FROMHOST-IP=='192.168.1.4'   then   ?RemoteLogs ?

Options:

A) *if $syslogfacility-text == 'remote' then ?RemoteLogs*

B) *if $fromhost-ip == '192.168.1.4' then ?RemoteLogs*

C) *if $hostname == '192.168.1.4' then ?RemoteLogs*

D) *if $msg contains 'RemoteLogs' then ?RemoteLogs*

A) *if $syslogfacility-text == 'remote' then ?RemoteLogs*

B) *if $fromhost-ip == '192.168.1.4' then ?RemoteLogs*

((Correct))

C) *if $hostname == '192.168.1.4' then ?RemoteLogs*

D) *if $msg contains 'RemoteLogs' then ?RemoteLogs*

Explanation

- Property-based filters in rsyslog are typically based on properties like `$fromhost-ip`.

- The provided expression translates to a property-based filter that checks if the `FROMHOST-IP` property is equal to '192.168.1.4' and then proceeds to the action `?RemoteLogs`.

Note

Expression-based filters offer more advanced capabilities for complex filtering logic, while Property-based filters provide a straightforward approach based on specific properties of log messages.

Question 53:

omusrmsg is an rsyslog built-in module that facilitates notifying users (it sends log messages to the user terminal). Write a rule to send all emergency messages of all facilities to both root and the regular user carol.

Options:

A) `` `*.emerg /dev/root, /dev/tty1` ``

B) `` `*.emerg @root, @carol` ``

C) `` `*.emerg /dev/tty1, /dev/pts/0` ``

D) `` `*.emerg /dev/null` ``

A) `` `*.emerg /dev/root, /dev/tty1` ``

B) `` `*.emerg @root, @carol` ``

C) `` `*.emerg /dev/tty1, /dev/pts/0` ``

((Correct))

D) `` `*.emerg /dev/null` ``

Explanation

- The `` `*.emerg` `` selector matches all emergency messages of all facilities.

- `` `/dev/tty1` `` represents the root terminal, and `` `/dev/pts/0` `` represents carol's terminal.

- Therefore, the rule `` `*.emerg /dev/tty1, /dev/pts/0` `` sends all emergency messages to both root and the regular user carol.

Question 54:

Which MTA is known for its flexibility but is considered more complex to configure compared to other options?

A) Postfix

B) Exim

C) Sendmail

((**Correct**))

D) qmail

Explanation

Sendmail is a widely used MTA known for its flexibility, but its configuration can be complex, especially for beginners.

Question 55:

What is the purpose of the `mailq` command in a Unix-like operating system?

A) To send email messages

B) To list the contents of the user's mailbox

C) To display the status of the email queue

((**Correct**))

D) To configure email forwarding rules

Explanation

The `mailq` command is used to view the status of the MTA's email queue, listing messages waiting to be delivered or processed.

Question 56:

What is the purpose of the lpoptions command in CUPS?

A) To set default printer options

((Correct))

B) To list available printers

C) To submit print jobs

D) To enable printer sharing

Explanation

The lpoptions command is used to set default printer options in CUPS.

Question 57:

Which command is used to submit a print job to a printer's queue?

A) lpr

((Correct))

B) lpadmin

C) lpq

D) lpstat

Explanation

The lpr command is used to submit a print job to a printer's queue in CUPS.

Question 58:

What is the purpose of the cupsreject command in CUPS?

A) To list available printers

B) To cancel print jobs

C) To reject new print jobs to a printer

((Correct))

D) To enable printer sharing

Explanation

The cupsreject command is used to reject new print jobs to a printer in CUPS.

Question 59:

How does IPv6 differ from IPv4 in terms of address representation?

A) IPv6 addresses are 64 bits long, while IPv4 addresses are 32 bits long

B) IPv6 addresses are represented in hexadecimal, while IPv4 addresses are represented in decimal

C) IPv6 addresses have a larger address space compared to IPv4

((Correct))

D) IPv6 addresses do not require subnetting, unlike IPv4 addresses

Explanation

IPv6 addresses are 128 bits long, providing a significantly larger address space compared to the 32-bit IPv4 addresses.

Question 60:

What is the primary function of a network mask (netmask)?

A) To encrypt data transmitted over the network

B) To identify the default gateway

C) To determine the range of IP addresses within a network

D) To determine which portion of an IP address is the network portion

((Correct))

Explanation

A network mask is used to identify the network portion of an IP address, separating it from the host portion.

Question 61:

Using the IP 172.16.30.230 and netmask 255.255.255.224, identify:

- The CIDR notation for the netmask

- Network address

- Broadcast address

- Number of IPs that can be used for hosts in this subnet

Options:

A) CIDR notation: /27, Network address: 172.16.30.224, Broadcast address: 172.16.30.255, Number of IPs: 30

B) CIDR notation: /26, Network address: 172.16.30.192, Broadcast address: 172.16.30.255, Number of IPs: 62

C) CIDR notation: /28, Network address: 172.16.30.192, Broadcast address: 172.16.30.223, Number of IPs: 32

D) CIDR notation: /27, Network address: 172.16.30.192, Broadcast address: 172.16.30.255, Number of IPs: 32

A) CIDR notation: /27, Network address: 172.16.30.224, Broadcast address: 172.16.30.255, Number of IPs: 30

((Correct))

B) CIDR notation: /26, Network address: 172.16.30.192, Broadcast address: 172.16.30.255, Number of IPs: 62

C) CIDR notation: /28, Network address: 172.16.30.192, Broadcast address: 172.16.30.223, Number of IPs: 32

D) CIDR notation: /27, Network address: 172.16.30.192, Broadcast address: 172.16.30.255, Number of IPs: 32

Explanation

The CIDR notation is determined by the number of leading 1 bits in the netmask. The network address is obtained by applying the bitwise AND operation between the IP and the netmask. The broadcast address is obtained by setting all host bits to 1 in the network address. The number of usable IPs for hosts is calculated by subtracting 2 (network and broadcast addresses) from the total number of addresses in the subnet.

Question 62:

Which setting is required on a host to allow an IP communication with a host in a different logical network? Options:

A) Default gateway

((Correct))

B) Subnet mask

C) MAC address

D) DNS server

Explanation

The default gateway is used to route traffic from a host to destinations outside of its local network.

Question 63:

Why are the IP ranges starting with 127 and the range after 224 not included in the IP address classes A, B or C? Options:

A) They are reserved for loopback and multicast addresses respectively

((Correct))

B) They are reserved for private networks

C) They are reserved for broadcast addresses

D) They are reserved for special-purpose addresses

Explanation

The IP range starting with 127 is reserved for loopback addresses, and the range after 224 is reserved for multicast addresses.

Question 64:

How could the hostnamectl command be used to change only the static hostname of the local machine to firewall? Options:

A) `hostnamectl set-hostname firewall`

((Correct))

B) `hostnamectl set-static-hostname firewall`

C) `hostnamectl set-local-hostname firewall`

D) `hostnamectl set-persistent-hostname firewall`

Explanation

The command `hostnamectl set-hostname firewall` changes the static hostname of the local machine to "firewall".

Question 65:

What details other than hostnames can be modified by command hostnamectl? Options:

A) Timezone, Kernel version

B) DNS server, Gateway

C) System locale, Icon theme

((Correct))

D) Chassis type, Boot loader

Explanation

Besides hostname, the `hostnamectl` command can be used to modify system locale and icon theme.

Question 66:

What entry in /etc/hosts associates both names firewall and router with IP 10.8.0.1? Options:

A) `10.8.0.1 router firewall`

B) `10.8.0.1 firewall router`

((Correct))

C) `router firewall 10.8.0.1`

D) `firewall router 10.8.0.1`

Explanation

The entry `10.8.0.1 firewall router` in `/etc/hosts` associates both "firewall" and "router" with the IP address 10.8.0.1.

Question 67:

How could the /etc/resolv.conf file be modified in order to send all DNS requests to 1.1.1.1? Options:

A) Add the line `nameserver 1.1.1.1` to /etc/resolv.conf

((Correct))

B) Add the line `1.1.1.1` to /etc/resolv.conf

C) Edit the line `search` to `1.1.1.1` in /etc/resolv.conf

D) Change the file permissions of /etc/resolv.conf to allow DNS requests to 1.1.1.1

Explanation

By adding the line `nameserver 1.1.1.1` to `/etc/resolv.conf`, DNS requests will be sent to the DNS server at IP address 1.1.1.1.

Question 68:

What is the primary purpose of NetworkManager in Linux?

A) To make network configuration as complex as possible

B) To automate network configuration and management

((**Correct**))

C) To only manage wired connections

D) To prioritize wireless connections over wired connections

Explanation

NetworkManager aims to simplify and automate network configuration, including DHCP setup, route changes, and DNS updates, making it easier for users to manage network connections.

Question 69:

Which command can be used to list available wireless networks in Linux using nmcli?

A) `ifconfig`

B) `iwlist`

C) `nmcli device wifi list`

((**Correct**))

D) `netstat`

Explanation

The `nmcli device wifi list` command is used to list available wireless networks in Linux when using NetworkManager.

Question 70:

How can you connect to a wireless network named "Hypnotoad" with a password "MyPassword" using nmcli in a graphical environment?

A) `nmcli connect Hypnotoad`

B) `nmcli device wifi connect Hypnotoad password MyPassword`

((**Correct**))

C) `nmcli wifi connect Hypnotoad MyPassword`

D) `nmcli device connect Hypnotoad`

Explanation

To connect to a wireless network using nmcli in a graphical environment, you need to specify the network name and password using the `nmcli device wifi connect` command.

Question 71:

Which command is used to deactivate a specific connection named "Hypnotoad" in NetworkManager?

A) `nmcli connection deactivate Hypnotoad`

B) `nmcli down Hypnotoad`

C) `nmcli connection down Hypnotoad`

((**Correct**))

D) `nmcli connection deactivate 6fdec048-bcc5-490a-832b-da83d8cb7915`

Explanation

The `nmcli connection down Hypnotoad` command is used to deactivate a specific connection named "Hypnotoad" in NetworkManager.

Question 72:

Which commands can be used to list network interfaces?

A) ifconfig, ping

B) ip addr, iwconfig

C) route, arp

D) ip link, ifconfig

((**Correct**))

Explanation

The `ip link` and `ifconfig` commands are commonly used to list network interfaces.

Question 73:

How would you temporarily disable an interface? How would you re-enable it?

A) `ifdown eth0`, `ifup eth0`

B) `ip disable eth0`, `ip enable eth0`

C) `ifconfig eth0 down`, `ifconfig eth0 up`

((**Correct**))

D) `ip down eth0`, `ip up eth0`

Explanation

To temporarily disable an interface, you can use `ifconfig INTERFACE down`, and to re-enable it, you can use `ifconfig INTERFACE up`.

Question 74:

Which of the following is a reasonable subnet mask for IPv4?

A) 0.0.0.255

B) 255.0.255.0

((Correct))

C) 255.252.0.0

D) /24

Explanation

Among the options provided, `255.0.255.0` is a valid subnet mask for IPv4 networks.

Question 75:

Which commands can you use to verify your default route?

A) `route`

B) `ip route`

C) `netstat -r`

D) All of the above

((Correct))

Explanation

All of the listed commands (`route`, `ip route`, `netstat -r`) can be used to verify the default route.

Question 76:

How would you add a second IP address to an interface?

A) `ip addr add ADDRESS dev INTERFACE`

((Correct))

B) `ifconfig INTERFACE add ADDRESS`

C) `ip addr add ADDRESS/24 dev INTERFACE`

D) `ifconfig INTERFACE ADDRESS`

Explanation

The `ip addr add ADDRESS dev INTERFACE` command is used to add a secondary IP address to a network interface.

Question 77:

Which subcommand of ip can be used to configure vlan tagging?

A) ip link

B) ip vlan

((Correct))

C) ip tag

D) ip vconfig

Explanation

The `ip vlan` subcommand is used to configure VLAN tagging.

Question 78:

What is the purpose of the 'nameserver' option in the /etc/resolv.conf file?

A) To specify the local domain name

B) To specify the IPv4 or IPv6 address of a DNS server

((Correct))

C) To set resolver options

D) To specify search domains

Explanation

The 'nameserver' option in /etc/resolv.conf is used to specify the IPv4 or IPv6 address of a DNS server.

Question 79:

What is the purpose of the 'search' option in the /etc/resolv.conf file?

A) To specify the local domain name

B) To specify the IPv4 or IPv6 address of a DNS server

C) To set resolver options

D) To specify search domains

((Correct))

Explanation

The 'search' option in /etc/resolv.conf is used to specify search domains for host name resolution.

Question 80:

Which command is used to scan for open ports on a host or network?

A) `netstat`

B) `nmap`

((Correct))

C) `lsof`

D) `fuser`

Explanation

The `nmap` command is used for network exploration and port scanning.

Question 81:

Which option is used with the `passwd` command to view password aging information for a user?

A) `-a`

B) `-s`

C) `-l`

D) `-S`

((Correct))

Explanation

The `-S` option is used with the `passwd` command to view password aging information for a user.

Question 82:

Which command is used to lock a user's password?

A) `lock`

B) `passwd -l`

((Correct))

C) `usermod -L`

D) `chage -l`

Explanation

The `passwd -l` command is used to lock a user's password.

Question 83:

Which file is used to configure individual services managed by xinetd?

A) /etc/xinetd.conf

B) /etc/services

C) /etc/xinetd.d/

((Correct))

D) /etc/inetd.conf

Explanation

Individual service configurations for xinetd are stored in files within the /etc/xinetd.d/ directory.

Question 84:

How can you restart the xinetd service after making configuration changes?

A) systemctl reload xinetd

B) service xinetd restart

C) systemctl restart xinetd

((Correct))

D) restart xinetd

Explanation

systemctl restart xinetd restarts the xinetd service.

Question 85:

What command can be used to list all running services on a systemd-based system?

A) systemctl list-services

B) service --status-all

C) systemctl list-units --type service

((Correct))

D) ps -ef | grep service

Explanation

systemctl list-units --type service lists all running services on a systemd-based system.

Question 86:

What is the default directory for user-specific configuration and authentication information in SSH?

A) /etc/ssh/

B) /usr/local/ssh/

C) ~/.ssh/

((Correct))

D) /var/lib/ssh/

Explanation

The `~/.ssh/` directory is the default location for user-specific configuration and authentication information in SSH.

Question 87:

Which SSH authentication method allows users to log in without providing a password but using public keys instead?

A) Password-based authentication

B) Public key authentication

((Correct))

C) Host-based authentication

D) Challenge-response authentication

Explanation

Public key authentication allows users to log in without providing a password by using their corresponding private keys for authentication.

Question 88:

How can the previously locked account emma be unlocked?

A) Run `passwd -u emma`.

((Correct))

B) Edit `/etc/passwd` file to remove the `!` symbol from emma's password field.

C) Use `usermod -U emma`.

D) There is no way to unlock a locked account without root access.

Explanation

The `passwd -u emma` command unlocks the account emma

by removing the `!` symbol from her password field in the `/etc/shadow` file.

Question 89:

Previously the account emma had an expiration date set. How can the expiration date get set to never?

A) Run `chage -E -1 emma`.

((**Correct**))

B) Edit `/etc/passwd` file to remove the expiration date field for emma.

C) Use `usermod -e " emma`.

D) There is no way to remove the expiration date for an account.

Explanation

The `chage -E -1 emma` command sets the expiration date for the account emma to never expire.

Question 90:

Imagine the CUPS printing service handling print jobs is not needed on your server. How can you disable the service permanently? How can you check the appropriate port is not active anymore?

A) Run `systemctl disable cups` and check with `netstat -tuln` for port 631.

((**Correct**))

B) Edit `/etc/cups/cupsd.conf` to set `Listen 0.0.0.0:0` and check with `nmap localhost` for port 631.

C) Use `service cups stop` and check with `ps aux | grep cupsd` for any running cups processes.

D) There is no way to permanently disable the CUPS service.

Explanation

Disabling the CUPS service using `systemctl disable cups` ensures it doesn't start on boot, and checking with `netstat -tuln` confirms that port 631, used by CUPS, is no longer active.

PRACTICE TEST FOUR - LPIC-1 EXAM 102 VERSION: 5.0

90 questions | 2 hours | 90% correct required to pass

The LPIC-1 Exam 102 Version: 5.0 Practice Test is a comprehensive resource designed to prepare you for the LPIC-1 (Linux Professional Institute Certification) Exam 102. It includes practice questions that mimic the format and content of the actual test. Each **Question** comes with a detailed **Explanation** to help you understand the concepts better. This practice test is an excellent tool to harness the power of Linux and achieve LPIC-1 certification.

Question 1:

One of the fields belonging to an IP packet that is very important is TTL (Time To Live). What is the function of this field and how does it work? Options:

A) It specifies the maximum number of hops that a packet can take before being discarded, decreasing by one at each router

((Correct))

B) It specifies the maximum amount of time a packet can exist in the network, decreasing by one second at each router

C) It specifies the maximum number of packets allowed to travel simultaneously, increasing by one at each router

D) It specifies the maximum amount of bandwidth allocated to a packet, decreasing by one byte at each router

Explanation

TTL is used to prevent packets from circulating indefinitely in case of routing loops. It decreases by one at each router the packet passes through.

Question 2:

Explain the function of NAT and when it is used. Options:

A) NAT translates private IP addresses to public IP addresses to enable communication over the internet, and it is used in private network environments.

((Correct))

B) NAT translates public IP addresses to private IP addresses to enable communication over the internet, and it is used in public network environments.

C) NAT encrypts data packets to secure communication over the internet, and it is used in VPN connections.

D) NAT compresses data packets to reduce bandwidth usage over the internet, and it is used in high-speed networks.

Explanation

Network Address Translation (NAT) is used to map private IP

addresses to public IP addresses to allow devices in a private network to communicate with the internet using a single public IP address.

Question 3:

Which port is the default for the SMTP protocol? Options:

A) 21

B) 25

((Correct))

C) 53

D) 80

Explanation

Port 25 is the default port for the Simple Mail Transfer Protocol (SMTP), used for email transmission.

Question 4:

How many different ports are available in a system? Options:

A) 65,535

((Correct))

B) 1024

C) 1023

D) 65536

Explanation

In TCP/IP networking, ports are represented by 16-bit unsigned integers, allowing for a total of 65,535 ports.

Question 5:

Search for it with set and grep: Which command combination correctly searches for the variable mammal within the current shell environment?

A) `set | grep mammal`

((Correct))

B) `env | grep mammal`

C) `export | grep mammal`

D) `echo $mammal`

Explanation

Option A searches for the variable mammal within the current shell environment by using the `set` command to list all shell variables and piping the output to `grep` to filter for the variable name.

Question 6:

Search for it with env and grep: How can you search for the variable mammal across the entire environment?

A) `set | grep mammal`

B) `env | grep mammal`

((Correct))

C) `export | grep mammal`

D) `echo $mammal`

Explanation

Option B searches for the variable mammal across the entire environment by using the `env` command to list all environment variables and piping the output to `grep` to filter for the variable name.

Question 7:

Create, in two consecutive commands, an environment variable named BIRD whose value is penguin: Which commands create an environment variable named BIRD with the value "penguin"?

A)

BIRD=penguin

export BIRD

((Correct))

B)

BIRD=penguin

set BIRD

C)

set BIRD=penguin

D)

export BIRD=penguin

Explanation

Option A sets the value of the variable BIRD to "penguin" and then exports it to the environment using the `export` command.

Question 8:

Create, in a single command, an environment variable named NEW_BIRD whose value is yellow-eyed penguin: How can you create an environment variable named NEW_BIRD with the value "yellow-eyed penguin" in one command?

A) `export NEW_BIRD="yellow-eyed penguin"`

((Correct))

B) `set NEW_BIRD="yellow-eyed penguin"`

C) `NEW_BIRD="yellow-eyed penguin"`

D) `create NEW_BIRD="yellow-eyed penguin"`

Explanation

Option A creates the environment variable NEW_BIRD and assigns it the value "yellow-eyed penguin" in one command using the `export` keyword.

Question 9:

Assuming you are user2, create a folder named bin in your home directory: What command creates a directory named "bin" in the home directory of user2?

A) `mkdir bin`

B) `mkdir ~/bin`

((Correct))

C) `create bin`

D) `cd bin`

Explanation

Option B uses the `mkdir` command to create a directory named "bin" in the home directory of the current user (~ represents the home directory).

Question 10:

Type the command to add the ~/bin folder to your PATH so that it is the first directory bash searches for binaries: How do you add the "~/bin" folder to the beginning of the PATH environment variable?

A) `export PATH=~/bin:$PATH`

((Correct))

B) `export PATH=$PATH:~/bin`

C) `set PATH=~/bin:$PATH`

D) `set PATH=$PATH:~/bin`

Explanation

Option A adds the "~/bin" folder to the beginning of the PATH environment variable, ensuring that it is the first directory searched for binaries.

Question 11:

To guarantee the value of PATH remains unaltered across reboots, what piece of code — in the form of an if statement — would you put into ~/.profile? Which code snippet ensures that the PATH environment variable remains unchanged across reboots?

A)

if [-z "$BASH_VERSION"]; then

 # Set PATH for non-interactive login shells

export PATH=/bin:/usr/bin:/usr/local/bin:/usr/local/sbin

fi

B)

if [-n "$BASH_VERSION"]; then

 # Set PATH for non-interactive login shells

export PATH=/bin:/usr/bin:/usr/local/bin:/usr/local/sbin

fi

((Correct))

C)

if [-z "$BASH_VERSION"]; then

 # Set PATH for interactive login shells

export PATH=/bin:/usr/bin:/usr/local/bin:/usr/local/sbin

fi

D)

if [-n "$BASH_VERSION"]; then

 # Set PATH for interactive login shells

export PATH=/bin:/usr/bin:/usr/local/bin:/usr/local/sbin

fi

Explanation

Option B checks if the BASH_VERSION variable is non-empty,

indicating that the shell is Bash. Then, it sets the PATH variable only for non-interactive login shells, ensuring that it remains unchanged across reboots.

Question 12:

let: more than arithmetic expression evaluation:

Do a manpage or web search for let and its implications when setting variables and create a new local variable named my_val whose value is 10 — as a result of adding 5 and 5:

Which command sets the value of the variable my_val to 10 by adding 5 and 5?

A) `let my_val=5+5`

((Correct))

B) `let my_val=5*5`

C) `let my_val=5/5`

D) `let my_val=5-5`

Explanation

Option A uses the `let` command to perform arithmetic addition and set the value of the variable my_val to 10.

Question 13:

The result of a command in a variable? Of course, that is possible; it is called command substitution. Investigate it and study the following function named music_info:

music_info(){

latest_music=$(ls -l1t ~/Music | head -n 6)

echo -e "Your latest 5 music files:\n$latest_music"

}

A) `latest_music=$(ls -llt ~/Music| head -n 6)`

((Correct))

B) `latest_music="(ls -llt ~/Music| head -n 6)"`

C) `latest_music=((ls -llt ~/Music| head -n 6))`

D) `latest_music={(ls -llt ~/Music| head -n 6)}`

Explanation

Option A correctly uses command substitution to assign the result of the command `ls -llt ~/Music | head -n 6` to the variable latest_music.

Question 14:

What is the primary purpose of aliases in the shell environment?

A) To create custom environment variables

B) To substitute long commands with shorter versions

((Correct))

C) To define functions for repetitive tasks

D) To manage system startup scripts

Explanation

Aliases allow users to create shorthand versions of longer commands, making it more convenient to execute frequently used commands.

Question 15:

Which command is used to create an alias in the shell environment?

A) define

B) set_alias

C) alias

((Correct))

D) assign_alias

Explanation

The `alias` command is used to create aliases in the shell environment.

Question 16:

What is the purpose of using the `\` character before an alias in the shell environment?

A) To escape the alias and disable it temporarily

((Correct))

B) To make the alias permanent

C) To create a nested alias

D) To pass parameters to the alias

Explanation

Using the `\` character before an alias allows users to temporarily disable the alias and access the original command.

Question 17:

Which file is commonly used to store personal aliases in the shell environment?

A) ~/.bash_profile

B) ~/.aliases

C) ~/.bash_aliases

((Correct))

D) ~/.bashrc

Explanation

The ` ~/.bash_aliases ` file is commonly used to store personal aliases in the shell environment.

Question 18:

In Bash scripting, what does the ` mapfile ` command do?

A) Maps a function to an array.

B) Maps a file to an array.

((Correct))

C) Maps a variable to a file.

D) Maps a variable to an array.

Explanation

The ` mapfile ` command reads lines from the standard input into an indexed array variable.

Question 19:

Which option of the `rsync` command ensures that only modified file pieces are copied from the origin?

A) `-a`

((Correct))

B) `-r`

C) `-q`

D) `--delete`

Explanation

The `-a` option activates the archive mode in `rsync`, which ensures that only modified file pieces are copied from the origin.

Question 20:

What is the purpose of the `shopt` command in Bash scripting?

A) Sets shell options.

((Correct))

B) Executes a shell script.

C) Manipulates file permissions.

D) Searches for files.

Explanation

The `shopt` command is used to set or unset various shell options.

Question 21:

In a Bash script, what does the `-e` option of the `set` command do?

A) Enables extended globbing.

B) Exits immediately if a command exits with a non-zero status.

((Correct))

C) Enables case-insensitive matching.

D) Enables error reporting.

Explanation

The `-e` option of the `set` command exits immediately if a command exits with a non-zero status.

Question 22:

Which loop construct in Bash walks through a given list of items and executes the same set of commands on each item?

A) `for`

((Correct))

B) `until`

C) `while`

D) `if`

Explanation

The `for` loop walks through a given list of items and executes the same set of commands on each item.

Question 23:

Which construct in Bash is used to evaluate several values against a single variable and execute commands based on the result?

A) `if`

B) `case`

((Correct))

C) `for`

D) `while`

Explanation

The `case` construct evaluates several values against a single variable and executes commands based on the result.

Question 24:

What does the `-t` option of the `mapfile` command do in Bash scripting?

A) Terminates the `mapfile` command.

B) Trims leading whitespace from input lines.

C) Removes trailing newline character from each line.

((Correct))

D) Transfers files between directories.

Explanation

The `-t` option of the `mapfile` command removes the trailing newline character from each line read from the input.

Question 25:

How can a keyboard layout be modified during a running X session in Linux?

A) Using the localectl command

B) Editing the xorg.conf file

C) Running the setxkbmap command

((Correct))

D) Modifying the ~/.xsession-errors file

Explanation

The setxkbmap command is used to modify a keyboard layout during a running X session in Linux.

Question 26:

What is the purpose of the Wayland protocol in modern Linux distributions?

A) To replace the X Window System

((Correct))

B) To enhance the functionality of X server

C) To provide backward compatibility with older applications

D) To improve network connectivity for X clients

Explanation

The Wayland protocol is designed to replace the X Window System in modern Linux distributions.

Question 27:

Which environment variable is used to specify the Wayland display in Linux?

A) WAYLAND_DISPLAY

((Correct))

B) XWAYLAND_DISPLAY

C) DISPLAY

D) X_DISPLAY

Explanation

The WAYLAND_DISPLAY environment variable is used to specify the Wayland display in Linux.

Question 28:

How can a new /etc/X11/xorg.conf configuration file be generated on a Linux system?

A) Using the xorg-gen command

B) Running the Xorg -configure command

((Correct))

C) Editing the ~/.xsession-errors file

D) Running the xconfig command

Explanation

The Xorg -configure command is used to generate a new /etc/X11/xorg.conf configuration file on a Linux system.

Question 29:

What is the purpose of the InputClass section in X server configuration?

A) To configure a specific model of keyboard or mouse

B) To describe the physical monitor used

C) To group configurations for hardware devices

((Correct))

D) To tie the Monitor and Device sections together

Explanation

The InputClass section in X server configuration is used to group configurations for hardware devices such as keyboards and mice.

Question 30:

Which command is used to start an application on a specific screen in the X Window System?

A) startx

B) xrun

C) xstart

D) DISPLAY

((Correct))

Explanation

The DISPLAY environment variable is used to start an application on a specific screen in the X Window System.

Question 31:

How can users simulate a right mouse click in Gnome's Universal Access settings?

A) By pressing and holding the left mouse button

((Correct))

B) By pressing the Shift key

C) By clicking on the screen

D) By pressing the Caps Lock key

Explanation

In Gnome's Universal Access settings, users can simulate a right mouse click by pressing and holding the left mouse button.

Question 32:

What accessibility feature can assist users with reduced eyesight by zooming in on parts of the screen?

A) Sticky keys

B) Slow keys

C) Bounce keys

D) Screen magnifier

((Correct))

Explanation

The screen magnifier is an accessibility feature that can assist users with reduced eyesight by zooming in on parts of the screen, making it easier to see details.

Question 33:

What accessibility feature could help a user to alternate between open windows using the keyboard, considering that the user is unable to press the Alt and Tab keys at the same time? Options:

A) Sticky keys

((Correct))

B) Mouse keys

C) Bounce keys

D) Slow keys

Explanation

Option A is correct. Sticky keys allow users to press one key at a time for keyboard shortcuts that usually require simultaneous key presses, such as Alt + Tab to switch between open windows.

Question 34:

Remove only the developers group from the secondary groups of kevin. Options:

A) gpasswd -d kevin developers

((Correct))

B) deluser kevin developers

C) userdel -G developers kevin

D) usermod -G developers kevin

Explanation

Option A demonstrates the correct usage of the gpasswd command to remove the developers group from the secondary groups of the user kevin.

Question 35:

Set the password for the kevin user account. Options:

A) passwd kevin

((Correct))

B) chpasswd kevin

C) userpasswd kevin

D) setpasswd kevin

Explanation

Option A correctly identifies the passwd command as the appropriate tool for setting a user's password, followed by the username (kevin in this case).

Question 36:

Using the chage command, first check the expiry date of the kevin user account and then change it to December 31st, 2022. What other command can you use to change the expiration date of a user account? Options:

A) usermod -e

((Correct))

B) chuser -e

C) userexpiry -e

D) chpasswd -e

Explanation

Option A is the correct command (usermod -e) to change the expiration date of a user account. The chage command is used to view and modify user account aging information, including password expiry dates.

Question 37:

Add a new user account named emma with UID 1050 and set administrators as its primary group and developers and web-designers as its secondary groups. Options:

A) useradd -u 1050 -G administrators,developers,web-designers emma

B) useradd -g administrators -G developers,web-designers -u 1050 emma

((Correct))

C) useradd -u 1050 -G administrators -G developers -G web-designers emma

D) useradd -G administrators,developers,web-designers -u 1050 emma

Explanation

Option B correctly specifies the primary group (administrators) and secondary groups (developers and web-designers) for the new user account emma with the UID 1050.

Question 38:

Change the login shell of emma to /bin/sh. Options:

A) usermod -s /bin/sh emma

((**Correct**))

B) chsh /bin/sh emma

C) usershell /bin/sh emma

D) setshell /bin/sh emma

Explanation

Option A demonstrates the correct usage of the usermod command to change the login shell of a user account to /bin/sh.

Question 39:

Delete the emma and kevin user accounts and the administrators, developers, and web-designers groups. Options:

A) userdel emma kevin && groupdel administrators developers web-designers

B) userdel emma kevin && delgroup administrators developers web-designers

C) deluser emma kevin && groupdel administrators developers web-designers

((**Correct**))

D) deluser emma kevin && delgroup administrators developers web-designers

Explanation

Option C correctly combines the deluser command to delete user accounts (emma and kevin) with the groupdel command to delete groups (administrators, developers, and web-designers).

Question 40:

Create another scheduled job that executes the foobar.sh script every minute, redirecting the output to the output.log file in your home directory so that only standard error is sent to you by e-mail. Options:

A) * * * * * /path/to/foobar.sh > ~/output.log 2>&1

B) * * * * * /path/to/foobar.sh > ~/output.log

((Correct))

C) * * * * * /path/to/foobar.sh 2> ~/output.log

D) * * * * * /path/to/foobar.sh | tee ~/output.log

Explanation

Option B correctly schedules the job to run every minute, redirecting standard output to output.log in the user's home directory.

Question 41:

Look at the crontab entry of the newly created scheduled job. Why is it not necessary to specify the absolute path of the file in which the standard output is saved? And why can you use the ./foobar.sh command to execute the script? Options:

A) Because cron automatically redirects output to the user's mailbox, and the current directory is included in the PATH environment variable.

((Correct))

B) Because cron automatically redirects output to the /var/log/

cron.log file, and the current directory is included in the PATH environment variable.

C) Because cron automatically redirects output to the /var/log/ cron.log file, and the current directory is not included in the PATH environment variable.

D) Because cron automatically redirects output to the user's mailbox, and the current directory is not included in the PATH environment variable.

Explanation

Option A is correct because cron by default sends output via email to the user who owns the crontab, and the current directory is usually included in the PATH environment variable.

Question 42:

Edit the previous crontab entry by removing the output redirection and disable the first cron job you have created. Options:

A) Comment out the line with a #

((Correct))

B) Delete the line

C) Add the entry to /etc/cron.deny

D) Add the entry to /etc/cron.allow

Explanation

Option A is correct as commenting out the line with a # disables the cron job without deleting it.

Question 43:

How can you send the output and errors of your scheduled job to the emma user account via email? And how can you avoid sending the standard output and error via e-mail? Options:

A) * * * * * /path/to/foobar.sh 2>&1 | mail -s "Output" emma@example.com

((Correct))

B) * * * * * /path/to/foobar.sh 2> /dev/null | mail -s "Output" emma@example.com

C) * * * * * /path/to/foobar.sh > /dev/null 2>&1 | mail -s "Output" emma@example.com

D) * * * * * /path/to/foobar.sh | mail -s "Output" emma@example.com

Explanation

Option A correctly sends both standard output and error to the emma user via email. Option B sends only errors to emma, while option C sends nothing (redirects all output to /dev/null).

Question 44:

Execute the command ls -l /usr/bin/crontab. Which special bit is set and what is its meaning? Options:

A) Setuid (s) - It allows users to run the crontab command with the permissions of the file owner.

((Correct))

B) Setgid (s) - It allows users to run the crontab command with the permissions of the file group.

C) Sticky bit (t) - It allows users to run the crontab command with restricted permissions.

D) Regular file (-) - It indicates that /usr/bin/crontab is a standard executable file.

Explanation

Option A is correct. The setuid (s) bit allows the crontab command to be executed with the permissions of the file owner, which is necessary to edit the user's crontab file.

Question 45:

For each of the following time specifications, indicate which is valid and which is invalid for `at`:

1. **at 08:30 AM next week**

2. **at midday**

3. **at 01-01-2020 07:30 PM**

4. **at 21:50 01.01.20**

5. **at now +4 days**

6. **at 10:15 PM 31/03/2021**

7. **at tomorrow 08:30 AM**

1. Valid, 2. Invalid, 3. Valid, 4. Valid, 5. Valid, 6. Invalid, 7. Invalid

((Correct))

1. Invalid, 2. Invalid, 3. Valid, 4. Valid, 5. Valid, 6. Invalid, 7. Invalid

1. Valid, 2. Invalid, 3. Invalid, 4. Valid, 5. Valid, 6. Invalid, 7.

Invalid

1. Valid, 2. Invalid, 3. Valid, 4. Valid, 5. Valid, 6. Valid, 7. Invalid

Explanation

1. at 08:30 AM next week

Valid: This specifies a time for 08:30 AM next week.

2. at midday

Invalid: "midday" is not a valid time format.

3. at 01-01-2020 07:30 PM

Valid: This specifies a time for January 1st, 2020, at 07:30 PM.

4. at 21:50 01.01.20

Valid: This specifies a time for January 1st, 2020, at 21:50.

5. at now +4 days

Valid: This specifies a time 4 days from the current time.

6. at 10:15 PM 31/03/2021

Invalid: The date format should be in the format MM/DD/YYYY or DD-MM-YYYY.

7. at tomorrow 08:30 AM

Invalid: "tomorrow" is not a valid time specifier.

Question 46:

Which environment variable can be used to temporarily override all other locale settings in Linux?

A) LC_ALL

((**Correct**))

B) LANG

C) LC_TIME

D) LC_NUMERIC

Explanation

The LC_ALL environment variable can be used to temporarily override all other locale settings in Linux.

Question 47:

What is the purpose of daylight savings time in many regions?

A) To increase system security

B) To improve network performance

C) To adjust clocks by an hour during part of the year

((**Correct**))

D) To synchronize with international time standards

Explanation

Daylight savings time is implemented in many regions to adjust clocks by an hour during part of the year, typically to extend evening daylight.

Question 48:

What is the significance of using the Unicode encoding standard in modern operating systems?

A) It reduces system resource usage

B) It provides a unique number for every character, ensuring compatibility between platforms and languages

((Correct))

C) It enhances network security

D) It improves system stability

Explanation

The Unicode encoding standard provides a unique number for every character, ensuring compatibility between platforms, languages, and applications.

Question 49:

Which command is used to verify NTP status if using the `chrony` service?

A) `chronyc status`

((Correct))

B) `ntpstatus`

C) `chronycheck`

D) `ntpq -p`

Explanation

The `chronyc status` command is used to verify NTP status if using the `chrony` service in Linux.

Question 50:

What does the term "Stratum" refer to in the context of NTP?

A) The absolute difference between system time and NTP time

B) The number of hops to a computer with an attached

reference clock

((**Correct**))

C) The rate by which the system's clock would be wrong if chronyd is not correcting it

D) The total of the network path delays to the stratum computer from which the computer is being synced

Explanation

In the context of NTP, "Stratum" refers to the number of hops to a computer with an attached reference clock.

Question 51:

Which command is used to manually step the system clock in `chrony`?

A) `chronyc adjust`

B) `chronyc step`

C) `chronyc makestep`

((**Correct**))

D) `chronyc sync`

Explanation

The `chronyc makestep` command is used to manually step the system clock in `chrony` in Linux.

Question 52:

What is the primary purpose of systemd-journald?

A) To manage system units and targets.

B) To control the boot process and service management.

C) To create and maintain a structured and indexed journal for logging.

((**Correct**))

D) To configure storage and size settings for log files.

Explanation

systemd-journald is responsible for receiving logging information from various sources and creating a structured and indexed journal.

Question 53:

Which command is used to query the systemd journal?

A) systemctl status

B) ls

C) journalctl

((**Correct**))

D) less

Explanation

The journalctl command is used to query the systemd journal and retrieve logging information.

Question 54:

How can you print the most recent journal messages and continuously monitor new entries?

A) journalctl -r

B) journalctl -n 10

C) journalctl -f

((**Correct**))

D) journalctl -e

Explanation

The -f option in journalctl allows you to continuously monitor new journal entries as they are appended to the journal.

Question 55:

Which option allows you to filter journal messages based on severity/priority?

A) -n

B) -p

((**Correct**))

C) -k

D) -b

Explanation

The -p option in journalctl allows you to filter messages based on severity/priority.

Question 56:

How can you filter journal data to display messages from the current boot?

A) journalctl -b

((**Correct**))

B) journalctl -b -1

C) journalctl --since "today"

D) journalctl -u ssh.service

Explanation

The -b option in journalctl is used to display messages from the current boot.

Question 57:

Which option is used to navigate through matches in forward and backward searches while using journalctl?

A) N

((Correct))

B) Shift + N

C) /

D) ?

Explanation

The N key is used to navigate to the next occurrence of a match during searches in journalctl.

Question 58:

Which file is commonly used to configure email aliases in a Unix-like operating system?

A) /etc/mail/aliases

((Correct))

B) ~/.forward

C) /etc/postfix/main.cf

D) /etc/sendmail.cf

Explanation

The `/etc/mail/aliases` file is commonly used to configure email aliases, redirecting email messages to specific users or destinations.

Question 59:

What happens if an MTA is configured as an open relay?

A) It rejects all incoming email messages.

B) It forwards email messages to external addresses without proper authentication.

((Correct))

C) It encrypts all outgoing email messages.

D) It filters spam and malicious emails.

Explanation

An open relay MTA can be abused by attackers to send spam or malicious emails by bypassing proper authentication, posing security risks.

Question 60:

Which option is used with the lpadmin command to delete a printer?

A) -r

B) -x

((Correct))

C) -d

D) -l

Explanation

The -x option is used with the lpadmin command to delete a printer.

Question 61:

How can a user view all print jobs they have submitted in CUPS?

A) Using the lpoptions command

B) Using the lpq command

((Correct))

C) Using the lpstat command

D) Using the lpr command

Explanation

The lpq command is used to view all print jobs a user has submitted in CUPS.

Question 62:

Which command is used to move a print job from one print queue to another in CUPS?

A) lprm

B) lpmove

((Correct))

C) lpadmin

D) cancel

Explanation

The lpmove command is used to move a print job from one print queue to another in CUPS.

Question 63:

Which transport protocol ensures that all packets are delivered properly, verifying the integrity and the order of the packets? Options:

A) TCP

((Correct))

B) UDP

C) ICMP

D) HTTP

Explanation

Transmission Control Protocol (TCP) ensures reliable and ordered delivery of packets by providing mechanisms for error checking and packet sequencing.

Question 64:

In systemd-networkd, where are the configuration files for network interfaces located with the highest priority?

A) `/run/systemd/network`

B) `/lib/systemd/network`

C) `/etc/systemd/network`

((**Correct**))

D) `/usr/systemd/network`

Explanation

Configuration files in `/etc/systemd/network` have the highest priority in systemd-networkd, followed by files in `/run/systemd/network` and then `/lib/systemd/network`.

Question 65:

What suffix is used for configuration files in systemd-networkd to set low-level configurations for network interfaces?

A) .netdev

B) .link

((**Correct**))

C) .network

D) .config

Explanation

Configuration files ending in .link are used in systemd-networkd to set low-level configurations for network interfaces.

Question 66:

Which section in a systemd-networkd .network file defines the network interface to which the configuration refers?

A) [Network]

B) [Match]

((**Correct**))

C) [Interface]

D) [Configuration]

Explanation

The [Match] section inside a systemd-networkd .network file defines the network interface to which the configuration refers.

Question 67:

What command is used to create a credentials file for a password-protected wireless network in systemd-networkd?

A) `wpa_passphrase`

((**Correct**))

B) `wpa_supplicant`

C) `systemctl start wpa_supplicant`

D) `systemctl enable wpa_supplicant`

Explanation

The `wpa_passphrase` command is used to create a credentials file for a password-protected wireless network in systemd-networkd.

Question 68:

How can you start the association between a wireless adapter and an access point in systemd-networkd?

A) ` systemctl start wpa_supplicant@wlo1.service `

((Correct))

B) ` nmcli device wifi connect MyWifi password MyPassword `

C) ` wpa_passphrase MyWifi > /etc/wpa_supplicant/ wpa_supplicant-wlo1.conf `

D) ` systemctl start systemd-networkd.service `

Explanation

The ` systemctl start wpa_supplicant@wlo1.service ` command starts the association between a wireless adapter and an access point in systemd-networkd.

Question 69:

What suffix is used for systemd-networkd configuration files that define network addresses and routes?

A) .netdev

B) .link

C) .network

((Correct))

D) .conf

Explanation

Configuration files ending in .network are used in systemd-networkd to define network addresses and routes.

Question 70:

Which command can be used to reconnect a disconnected

network interface in NetworkManager?

A) `nmcli connection reconnect Hypnotoad`

B) `nmcli device connect wlo1`

C) `nmcli connection up Hypnotoad`

((Correct))

D) `nmcli device reconnect wlo1`

Explanation

The `nmcli connection up Hypnotoad` command can be used to reconnect a disconnected network interface in NetworkManager.

Question 71:

How can you turn off the wireless radio using nmcli?

A) `nmcli radio off`

((Correct))

B) `nmcli device wifi off`

C) `nmcli network off`

D) `nmcli device radio off`

Explanation

The `nmcli radio off` command is used to turn off the wireless radio using nmcli.

Question 72:

How would you configure a default route?

A) `route add default gw GATEWAY`

B) `ip route add default via GATEWAY`

C) `route add -default GATEWAY`

D) `ip route add default gw GATEWAY`

((**Correct**))

Explanation

The `ip route add default gw GATEWAY` command is used to configure a default route.

Question 73:

How would you get detailed information about the ip neighbour command? What happens if you run it by itself?

A) `man ip neighbour`; It displays a list of neighbor cache entries.

B) `ip neighbour help`; It shows detailed usage information for the command.

((**Correct**))

C) `ip neighbour info`; It provides detailed information about each neighbor entry.

D) `ip neighbour`; It displays a summary of neighbor cache entries.

Explanation

Running `ip neighbour` without arguments typically shows a summary of neighbor cache entries. To get detailed information, you would use `ip neighbour help`.

Question 74:

How would you backup your routing table? How would you restore from it?

A) Backup: `cp /etc/sysconfig/network-scripts/route-*` / backup/`; Restore: `cp /backup/route-* /etc/sysconfig/ network-scripts/`

B) Backup: `route > route_backup.txt`; Restore: `route < route_backup.txt`

C) Backup: `ip route > route_backup.txt`; Restore: `ip route < route_backup.txt`

((Correct))

D) Backup: `cat /proc/net/route > route_backup.txt`; Restore: `cat route_backup.txt > /proc/net/route`

Explanation

You can backup the routing table using `ip route > route_backup.txt`, and restore it using `ip route < route_backup.txt`.

Question 75:

Which ip subcommand can be used to configure spanning tree options?

A) ip link

B) ip route

C) ip stp

D) ip bridge

((Correct))

Explanation

The `ip bridge` subcommand can be used to configure spanning tree options for bridge devices.

Question 76:

What command(s) would you use to send an ICMP echo to learning.lpi.org?

A) `ping learning.lpi.org`

B) `traceroute learning.lpi.org`

C) `netcat learning.lpi.org`

D) `ping -c 4 learning.lpi.org`

((Correct))

Explanation

The `ping` command with the `-c` option allows you to specify the number of ICMP echo requests to send.

Question 77:

How could you determine the route to 8.8.8.8?

A) `ip route get 8.8.8.8`

B) `route -n get 8.8.8.8`

C) `traceroute 8.8.8.8`

D) All of the above

((Correct))

Explanation

All of the listed commands (`ip route get 8.8.8.8`, `route -n get 8.8.8.8`, `traceroute 8.8.8.8`) can be used to determine the route to a specific destination.

Question 78:

Which systemd service provides mDNS, DNS, and LLMNR functionality?

A) systemd-networkd

B) systemd-resolved

((Correct))

C) systemd-timesyncd

D) systemd-journald

Explanation

systemd-resolved provides mDNS, DNS, and LLMNR functionality in Linux.

Question 79:

Which command is used to display entries from name service databases in Linux?

A) host

B) dig

C) getent

((Correct))

D) nslookup

Explanation

The getent command is used to display entries from name service databases in Linux.

Question 80:

Which command is used to display all current soft limits on system resources?

A) `ulimit -s`

B) `ulimit -a`

((Correct))

C) `ulimit -l`

D) `ulimit -v`

Explanation

The `ulimit -a` command displays all current soft limits on system resources.

Question 81:

Which utility is used to change the password and account expiry information for a user?

A) `passwd`

B) `chpasswd`

C) `chage`

((Correct))

D) `usermod`

Explanation

The `chage` utility is used to change the password and account expiry information for a user.

Question 82:

Which command is used to switch to another user account during a login session?

A) `su`

((Correct))

B) `sudo`

C) `switch`

D) `user`

Explanation

The `su` command (short for "switch user") is used to switch to another user account during a login session. It prompts you to enter the password of the target user account unless you specify the username as an argument.

Question 83:

How can you disable unnecessary services on a systemd-based system?

A) systemctl disable <service>

((Correct))

B) chkconfig <service> off

C) update-rc.d <service> remove

D) service <service> disable

Explanation

systemctl disable <service> disables unnecessary services on a systemd-based system.

Question 84:

Which command can be used to check for listening network services on older systems?

A) netstat -ltu

((Correct))

B) ss -ltu

C) lsof -i :22

D) nmap localhost

Explanation

netstat -ltu checks for listening network services on older systems.

Question 85:

What technology was commonly used in the past as a simple firewall for securing network connections into a host?

A) iptables

B) nftables

C) TCP wrappers

((Correct))

D) SELinux

Explanation

TCP wrappers were commonly used in the past as a simple firewall for securing network connections into a host.

Question 86:

You have installed the nginx web server. How can you check whether nginx supports TCP wrappers?

A) Examine the `/etc/hosts.allow` and `/etc/hosts.deny` files for nginx entries.

B) Run `nginx -V` and check for `--with-cc-opt=-DNGX_TCP_WRAPPERS` in the output.

((Correct))

C) Use `tcpdchk` to analyze nginx configuration files.

D) There is no direct way to check if nginx supports TCP wrappers.

Explanation

The `nginx -V` command displays the compile-time options used to build nginx, and the presence of `-DNGX_TCP_WRAPPERS` indicates support for TCP wrappers.

Question 87:

What is the primary purpose of using GNU Privacy Guard (GPG) in Linux?

A) To compress files for storage efficiency

B) To encrypt and decrypt files securely

((Correct))

C) To manage user authentication in a network

D) To monitor system performance metrics

Explanation

GPG is primarily used for encrypting and decrypting files to ensure their security and confidentiality.

Question 88:

Which standard does GPG follow for encryption as defined by the Internet Engineering Task Force (IETF)?

A) SSL/TLS

B) PGP

C) OpenSSH

D) OpenPGP

((Correct))

Explanation

GPG follows the OpenPGP standard defined by the IETF for encryption and digital signatures.

Question 89:

What is the purpose of the private key in GPG encryption?

A) To encrypt messages

B) To decrypt messages

((Correct))

C) To distribute to others

D) To verify signatures

Explanation

The private key is used to decrypt messages that have been encrypted using the corresponding public key.

Question 90:

Which command is used to generate a new key pair in GPG?

A) gpg --gen-key

((**Correct**))

B) gpg --create-key

C) gpg --new-key

D) gpg --generate-key

Explanation

The command `gpg --gen-key` is used to generate a new key pair in GPG.

PRACTICE TEST FIVE - LPIC-1 EXAM 102 VERSION: 5.0

90 questions | 2 hours | 90% correct required to pass

The LPIC-1 Exam 102 Version: 5.0 Practice Test is a comprehensive resource designed to prepare you for the LPIC-1 (Linux Professional Institute Certification) Exam 102. It includes practice questions that mimic the format and content of the actual test. Each **Question** comes with a detailed **Explanation** to help you understand the concepts better. This practice test is an excellent tool to harness the power of Linux and achieve LPIC-1 certification.

Question 1:

What is the primary advantage of using functions over aliases in the shell environment?

A) Functions allow for dynamic command substitution

B) Functions are easier to define

C) Functions can include flow control structures

((Correct))

D) Functions have higher priority than aliases

Explanation

Functions in the shell environment offer more flexibility and can include flow control structures such as loops and conditionals.

Question 2:

Which special variable expands to the result of the last command run in the shell environment?

A) $$

B) $?

((Correct))

C) $@

D) $_

Explanation

The `$?` special variable expands to the result of the last command run in the shell environment, where a value of 0 means success.

Question 3:

What is the purpose of the `unset` command in the shell

environment?

A) To delete environment variables

B) To remove aliases and functions

((Correct))

C) To unset positional parameters

D) To disable special built-in variables

Explanation

The `unset` command in the shell environment is used to remove aliases and functions.

Question 4:

Which file is commonly used to define functions in the shell environment?

A) ~/.bash_profile

B) ~/.functions

C) ~/.bash_functions

D) ~/.bashrc

((Correct))

Explanation

Functions are commonly defined in the `~/.bashrc` file in the shell environment.

Question 5:

What is the purpose of using double quotes ("") in an alias definition in the shell environment?

GHADAATEF

A) To disable alias expansion

B) To enable parameter expansion

C) To make the expansion dynamic

((Correct))

D) To create nested aliases

Explanation

Double quotes ("") in an alias definition allow for dynamic expansion of variables and commands.

Question 6:

Which special variable expands to the number of arguments passed to a command in the shell environment?

A) $#

((Correct))

B) $@

C) $*

D) $_

Explanation

The `$#` special variable expands to the number of arguments passed to a command in the shell environment.

Question 7:

In which file should functions be defined to ensure persistence across system reboots in the shell environment?

A) ~/.bash_profile

B) /etc/bash.bashrc

C) ~/.functions

D) ~/.bashrc

((Correct))

Explanation

Functions should be defined in the `~/.bashrc` file to ensure persistence across system reboots in the shell environment.

Question 8:

How can an alias be invoked in the shell environment?

A) By using the `invoke` command followed by the alias name

B) By typing the alias name into the terminal

((Correct))

C) By using the `execute` command followed by the alias name

D) By specifying the alias name as an argument to the `alias` command

Explanation

Aliases can be invoked in the shell environment by simply typing the alias name into the terminal.

Question 9:

Considering the capabilities of aliases and functions, check if the provided information is True or False.

| Feature | Aliases? | Functions? |

| Local variables can be used | No | Yes |

| Environment variables can be used | No | Yes |

| Can be escaped with \ | No | Yes |

| Can be recursive | No | Yes |

| Very productive when used with positional parameters | Yes | Yes |

A) True

B) False

((Correct))

Explanation

1. Local variables can be used:

Aliases: True.

Functions: True. Functions in Bash allow the use of local variables, which are scoped to the function and not accessible outside of it.

2. Environment variables can be used:

Aliases: True.

Functions: True. Functions can access and modify environment variables as well as define their own local variables.

3. Can be escaped with \:

Aliases: True.

Functions: False.

4. Can be recursive:

Aliases: True.

Functions: True. Functions can call themselves recursively, allowing for complex and iterative tasks to be performed.

5. Very productive when used with positional parameters:

Aliases: False.

Functions: True. Functions are also productive when used with positional parameters, as they allow for the creation of reusable code blocks that can accept arguments.

Understanding the differences between aliases and functions in Bash is crucial for efficient shell scripting and command-line usage. While both aliases and functions provide ways to create shortcuts and custom commands, functions offer more flexibility and functionality, including the use of local variables, environment variables, recursion, and positional parameters.

Question 10:

Enter the command that lists all aliases in your system: Which command displays a list of all aliases defined in the current shell environment?

A) `alias`

((Correct))

B) `listaliases`

C) `showaliases`

D) `aliases`

Explanation

Option A correctly displays a list of all aliases defined in the current shell environment.

Question 11:

Write an alias named logg that lists all ogg files in ~/Music — one per line: Which command creates an alias named logg to list all ogg files in the directory ~/Music?

A) `alias logg="ls -1 ~/Music/*.ogg"`

((Correct))

B) `alias logg="ls ~/Music/*.ogg | grep -o '[^/]*$'"`

C) `alias logg="find ~/Music -type f -name '*.ogg'"`

D) `alias logg="ls -1 ~/Music/*.ogg | awk -F'/' '{print $NF}'"`

Explanation

Option A creates an alias named logg that uses the `ls` command to list all ogg files in the directory ~/Music, with each file on a separate line.

Question 12:

Invoke the alias to prove it works: How do you verify that the alias logg successfully lists all ogg files in ~/Music?

A) `logg`

((Correct))

B) `alias logg`

C) `logg ~/Music`

D) `execute logg`

Explanation

Option A directly invokes the alias logg to list all ogg files in ~/
Music.

Question 13:

Modify the alias `logg` so that it echoes out the session's user
and a colon before the listing: Which modification correctly
adds the session user and a colon before the listing of ogg files
in the logg alias?

A) `alias logg="echo $USER: ; ls -1 ~/Music/*.ogg"`

B) `alias logg="echo $(whoami): ; ls -1 ~/Music/*.ogg"`

((Correct))

C) `alias logg="echo $(whoami) ; ls -1 ~/Music/*.ogg"`

D) `alias logg="echo $USER ; ls -1 ~/Music/*.ogg"`

Explanation

Option B correctly modifies the logg alias to echo the session
user (using `whoami`) followed by a colon before listing the
ogg files.

Question 14:

Invoke the alias `logg` again to prove this new version also
works: How do you confirm that the modified logg alias
successfully echoes the session user and lists the ogg files?

A) `alias logg`

B) `logg`

((Correct))

C) `echo logg`

D) `logg | echo`

Explanation

Option B directly invokes the logg alias to demonstrate that it successfully echoes the session user and lists the ogg files.

Question 15:

List all aliases and check if the logg alias appears in the listing: Which command verifies whether the logg alias is included in the list of aliases?

A) `listaliases`

B) `aliases`

C) `alias`

((Correct))

D) `alias logg`

Explanation

Option C lists all defined aliases, allowing you to check if the logg alias appears in the listing.

Question 16:

Remove the `logg` alias: How do you remove the logg alias?

A) `remove logg`

B) `delete logg`

C) `unalias logg`

((Correct))

D) `unset logg`

Explanation

Option C removes the logg alias using the `unalias` command.

Question 17:

Which command is used to enable case-insensitive pattern matching in Bash scripts?

A) `shopt -u nocasematch`

B) `shopt -s nocasematch`

((Correct))

C) `shopt -u caseinsensitive`

D) `shopt -s caseinsensitive`

Explanation

The `shopt -s nocasematch` command is used to enable case-insensitive pattern matching in Bash scripts.

Question 18:

Login to the system as an ordinary user and create an at job that runs the bar.sh script tomorrow at 10:00 AM. Assume the script is located in the user's home directory.

A) echo "/home/user/bar.sh" | at 10:00 AM tomorrow

((Correct))

B) echo "sh /home/user/bar.sh" | at 10:00 AM tomorrow

C) echo "bash /home/user/bar.sh" | at 10:00 AM tomorrow

D) echo "/home/user/bar.sh" | at now + 1 day 10:00

Explanation

The correct answer is **A) echo "/home/user/bar.sh" | at 10:00 AM tomorrow**.

A) echo "/home/user/bar.sh" | at 10:00 AM tomorrow: This command echoes the path to the bar.sh script and pipes it to the at command, scheduling it to run at 10:00 AM the next day.

B) echo "sh /home/user/bar.sh" | at 10:00 AM tomorrow: This command echoes a command to execute the script using sh and pipes it to the at command. However, specifying the shell explicitly is unnecessary and could lead to unexpected behavior.

C) echo "bash /home/user/bar.sh" | at 10:00 AM tomorrow: Similar to option B, this command echoes a command to execute the script using bash. Again, specifying the shell explicitly is unnecessary.

D) echo "/home/user/bar.sh" | at now + 1 day 10:00: This command uses the now + 1 day syntax to schedule the job for tomorrow, but it does not specify the exact time (10:00 AM), which is required.

Detailed Explanation:

The at command is used to schedule commands or scripts to run at a specified time in the future. To schedule the execution of a script, you typically use echo to specify the command to be executed and pipe it to the at command.

In this scenario, the correct command to schedule the bar.sh script to run tomorrow at 10:00 AM for an ordinary user logged into the system is:

$ echo "/home/user/bar.sh" | at 10:00 AM tomorrow

This command echoes the path to the script (/home/user/bar.sh) and pipes it to the at command, specifying the time (10:00 AM) and the keyword tomorrow to schedule it for execution on the following day.

Understanding how to use the at command to schedule jobs is essential for automating tasks on Linux systems. It provides a simple yet powerful way to execute commands or scripts at specific times, aiding in task automation and management.

Question 19:

As an ordinary user, create an at job that runs the bar.sh script tomorrow at 10:00 AM. Assuming the script is located in the user's home directory: echo "~/bar.sh" | at 10:00 AM tomorrow

A) (Correct)

((Correct))

B) Not **(Correct)**

Explanation

The correct answer is **A) (Correct)**.

The command provided:

$ echo "~/bar.sh" | at 10:00 AM tomorrow

is correct for scheduling the bar.sh script to run tomorrow at 10:00 AM. Let's break down the command:

echo "~/bar.sh": This command echoes the path to the bar.sh script. The tilde (~) represents the user's home directory. However, using quotes (") around ~ prevents it from being expanded to the actual home directory path. To specify the home directory, it's better to use $HOME instead.

| at 10:00 AM tomorrow: This pipes the echoed path to the at command, specifying that the command should be executed at 10:00 AM tomorrow.

Therefore, the command provided correctly schedules the execution of bar.sh script for 10:00 AM the next day.

Understanding how to use the at command is crucial for scheduling tasks or scripts to run at specific times in Linux systems. In this scenario, the command provided effectively schedules the execution of the bar.sh script for an ordinary user, demonstrating proficiency in task automation on Linux systems.

Question 20:

Based on the following output of the command ` date `, what is the time zone of the system in GMT notation?

$ date

Mon Oct 21 18:45:21 +05 2019

Options:

A) GMT+5

B) GMT+4

C) GMT-5

D) GMT-4

A) GMT+5

((Correct))

B) GMT+4

C) GMT-5

D) GMT-4

Explanation

The `date` command displays the time zone offset, which is +05 in this case, indicating a time zone of GMT+5.

Question 21:

To what file should the symbolic link `/etc/localtime` point to in order to make Europe/Brussels the system's default local time? Options:

A) `/usr/share/zoneinfo/Europe/Brussels`

((Correct))

B) `/etc/zoneinfo/Europe/Brussels`

C) `/usr/local/zoneinfo/Europe/Brussels`

D) `/etc/timezone/Europe/Brussels`

Explanation

The symbolic link `/etc/localtime` should point to the time zone file in the zoneinfo directory, which is typically located at `/usr/share/zoneinfo/Europe/Brussels`.

Question 22:

Characters in text files may not be rendered correctly in a system with a character encoding different from that used in the text document. How could `iconv` be used to convert the WINDOWS-1252 encoded file `old.txt` to the file `new.txt` using UTF-8 encoding? Options:

A) `iconv -f WINDOWS-1252 -t UTF-8 old.txt > new.txt`

((Correct))

B) `iconv -f UTF-8 -t WINDOWS-1252 old.txt > new.txt`

C) `iconv -f WINDOWS-1252 -t UTF-8 new.txt > old.txt`

D) `iconv -f UTF-8 -t WINDOWS-1252 new.txt > old.txt`

Explanation

Option A is correct. It specifies the source encoding `-f WINDOWS-1252` and the target encoding `-t UTF-8`, followed by the input file `old.txt` and output redirection to `new.txt`.

Question 23:

Indicate whether the following commands related to displaying or modifying system time or hardware time are True or False:

Command(s)	System	Hardware	Both
`date -u`	Yes	No	No
`hwclock --set --date "12:00:00"`	No	Yes	No
`timedatectl`	Yes	No	No
`timedatectl	grep RTC`	Yes	No	No
`hwclock --hctosys`	No	Yes	No
`date +%T -s "08:00:00"`	Yes	No	No
`timedatectl settime 1980-01-10`	Yes	No	No

A) True

B) False

((Correct))

240

Explanation

1. date -u:

System: True. This command displays the system time in Coordinated Universal Time (UTC), also known as Greenwich Mean Time (GMT).

Hardware: False. This command does not interact with hardware time.

Both: False. While it displays system time, it does not modify either system or hardware time.

2. hwclock --set --date "12:00:00":

System: False. This command sets the hardware clock (hwclock), not the system time.

Hardware: True. This command sets the hardware clock to the specified time.

Both: False. It only modifies the hardware clock.

3. timedatectl:

System: True. This command displays and modifies system time and related settings.

Hardware: True.

Both: True.

4. timedatectl | grep RTC:

System: False.

Hardware: True.

Both: False.

5. hwclock --hctosys:

System: True.

Hardware: False.

Both: False.

6. date +%T -s "08:00:00":

System: True. This command sets the system time to 08:00:00.

Hardware: False. It does not interact with hardware time.

Both: False. It only modifies the system time.

7. timedatectl settime 1980-01-10:

System: True. This command sets the system time to January 10, 1980.

Hardware: True.

Both: True.

Understanding the functionality of commands related to system and hardware time is essential for managing time settings effectively in Linux systems. These commands provide various options for displaying, setting, and synchronizing system and hardware time, contributing to system stability and accuracy.

Question 24:

Observe the following output, and then correct the format of the argument so that the command is successful:

$ date --debug --date "20/20/12 0:10 -3"

date: warning: value 20 has less than 4 digits. Assuming MM/DD/ YY[YY] date: parsed date part: (Y-M-D) 0002-20-20

date: parsed time part: 00:10:00 UTC-03

date: input timezone: parsed date/time string (-03)

date: using specified time as starting value: '00:10:00'

date: error: invalid date/time value:

date: user provided time: '(Y-M-D) 0002-20-20 00:10:00 TZ=-03'

date: normalized time: '(Y-M-D) 0003-08-20 00:10:00 TZ=-03'

date: ---- --

date: possible reasons:

date: numeric values overflow;

date: incorrect timezone

date: invalid date '20/20/2 0:10 -3'

Which of the following correctly formats the date argument to ensure the command is successful?

A) date --debug --date "20/12/20 00:10:00 -03:00"

((Correct))

B) date --debug --date "20-12-20 00:10:00 -03:00"

C) date --debug --date "2020/12/20 00:10:00 -03:00"

D) date --debug --date "12/20/20 00:10:00 -03:00"

Explanation

The correct format for the date argument to ensure the command is successful is:

A) date --debug --date "20/12/20 00:10:00 -03:00"

This format represents December 20, 2020, with the time 00:10:00 and the timezone offset of UTC-03:00.

The date is provided in the format MM/DD/YY or YY/MM/DD, followed by the time separated by colons (:), and the timezone offset specified with the format ±HH:MM.

Option B is incorrect because it uses dashes - instead of slashes / to separate the date components, which may cause parsing errors.

Option C is incorrect because it includes the year with four digits (2020), which is not consistent with the warning about less than four digits.

Option D is incorrect because it starts with the month (12), followed by the day (20), and then the year (20), which is not consistent with the warning about less than four digits.

Therefore, option A is the correct choice for formatting the date argument to ensure the command is successful.

Understanding the correct syntax for specifying dates, times, and timezones is essential for using the date command effectively in Linux systems. Proper formatting ensures accurate interpretation and manipulation of dates and times, contributing to reliable system administration tasks.

Question 25:

What command will make Pacific/Auckland the default time zone for the current shell session? Options:

A) `export TZ=Pacific/Auckland`

((Correct))

B) `setenv TZ Pacific/Auckland`

C) `TZ=Pacific/Auckland`

D) `set TZ=Pacific/Auckland`

Explanation

Option A correctly sets the `TZ` environment variable to `Pacific/Auckland` for the current shell session.

Question 26:

What does the --vacuum-time option in journalctl do?

A) Deletes archived journal files based on a specified size.

B) Deletes archived journal files older than a specified timeframe.

((Correct))

C) Merges entries from all available journals.

D) Flushes journal files from runtime to persistent storage.

Explanation

The --vacuum-time option in journalctl is used to delete archived journal files that are older than a specified timeframe.

Question 27:

Which option in journald.conf controls the maximum size to which individual journal files can grow?

A) MaxRetentionSec

B) MaxFileSize

((Correct))

C) SystemMaxUse

D) SystemKeepFree

Explanation

The MaxFileSize option in journald.conf controls the maximum size to which individual journal files can grow.

Question 28:

What is the default behavior if /var/log/journal/ does not exist?

A) Log data will be stored persistently in /var/log/journal/.

B) Log data will be stored in memory under /run/log/journal/.

((Correct))

C) Log data will be discarded.

D) Log data will be forwarded to other targets such as the console or syslog.

Explanation

If /var/log/journal/ does not exist, log data will be stored in memory under /run/log/journal/.

Question 29:

How can you forward log data from the journal to a traditional syslog daemon?

A) By enabling the ForwardToKMsg option.

B) By forwarding messages to the socket file /run/systemd/journal/syslog.

((Correct))

C) By using the --flush option with journalctl.

D) By vacuuming archived journal files.

Explanation

Log data from the journal can be made available to a traditional syslog daemon by forwarding messages to the socket file /run/systemd/journal/syslog.

Question 30:

What command is used to clean archived journal files based on a specified size?

A) journalctl --vacuum-time

B) journalctl --vacuum-size

((Correct))

C) journalctl --vacuum-files

D) journalctl --rotate

Explanation

The journalctl --vacuum-size command is used to clean archived journal files based on a specified size.

Question 31:

Which option in journald.conf controls the amount of disk space that can be taken up by the journal?

A) MaxRetentionSec

B) MaxUse

((Correct))

C) SystemKeepFree

D) MaxFiles

Explanation

The MaxUse option in journald.conf controls the amount of disk space that can be taken up by the journal.

Question 32:

Which command is used to update the MTA's aliases database after modifying the /etc/aliases file?

A) newaliases

((Correct))

B) mailq

C) sendmail -bi

D) mail

Explanation

The `newaliases` command is used to update the MTA's aliases database after making changes to the `/etc/aliases` file.

Question 33:

Which protocol is commonly used by email client applications to retrieve messages from a remote server?

A) SMTP

B) POP3

C) IMAP

((Correct))

D) SSH

Explanation

IMAP (Internet Message Access Protocol) is commonly used by email client applications to retrieve messages from a remote server while keeping them synchronized across multiple devices.

Question 34:

A new printer was just installed on a local workstation named office-mgr. What command could be used to set this printer as the default for this workstation? Options:

A) `lpadmin -d office-mgr`

((Correct))

B) `lpoptions -d office-mgr`

C) `lp -d office-mgr`

D) `lpoptions -d default=office-mgr`

Explanation

The `lpadmin -d office-mgr` command is used to set the default printer to office-mgr.

Question 35:

Which command and option would be used to determine what printers are available for printing from a workstation? Options:

A) `lpq -a`

B) `lpstat -p`

C) `lpoptions -l`

D) `lpstat -a`

((Correct))

Explanation

The `lpstat -a` command is used to display all available printers.

Question 36:

Using the cancel command, how would you remove a print job with ID 15 that is stuck in the queue for the printer named office-mgr? Options:

A) `cancel 15`

B) `cancel office-mgr 15`

((Correct))

C) `cancel -H office-mgr 15`

D) `cancel -u office-mgr 15`

Explanation

The `cancel` command followed by the printer name and job ID is used to remove a specific print job from the queue.

Question 37:

Which type of IPv6 address is used to sent a packet to all interfaces that belong to group of hosts? Options:

A) Unicast

B) Multicast

((Correct))

C) Anycast

D) Broadcast

Explanation

IPv6 multicast addresses are used to send packets to multiple interfaces, belonging to a group of hosts identified by a single multicast address.

Question 38:

Mention 4 examples of services that use the TCP protocol by default. Options:

A) SSH, FTP, HTTP, Telnet

((Correct))

B) DNS, DHCP, SNMP, TFTP

C) SMTP, POP3, IMAP, SNMP

D) FTP, TFTP, HTTP, DNS

Explanation

SSH (Secure Shell), FTP (File Transfer Protocol), HTTP (Hypertext Transfer Protocol), and Telnet are examples of services that use TCP by default for reliable data transmission.

Question 39:

What is the name of the field on IPv6 header package that implement the same resource of TTL on IPv4? Options:

A) Hop Limit

((Correct))

B) Time To Live

C) Time To Destination

D) Destination Limit

Explanation

The "Hop Limit" field in the IPv6 header serves the same purpose as the "Time To Live" (TTL) field in IPv4, determining the maximum number of hops a packet can traverse before being discarded.

Question 40:

What kind of information Neighbor Discovery Protocol (NDP) is able to discover? Options:

A) MAC addresses and link-local addresses

B) IP addresses and MAC addresses

((Correct))

C) Subnet masks and default gateways

D) DNS server addresses and DHCP lease durations

Explanation

NDP is part of the ICMPv6 protocol suite used in IPv6 networks to discover various information, including IP addresses and MAC addresses of neighboring nodes on the same link.

Question 41:

What is the meaning of the word Portal in the CONNECTIVITY column in the output of command nmcli general status?

Options:

A) The device is connected to a captive portal network.

((Correct))

B) The device is connected to a VPN.

C) The device is connected to a mesh network.

D) The device is connected to a virtual private network.

Explanation

In the context of the `nmcli` command, "Portal" in the CONNECTIVITY column indicates that the device is connected to a network with a captive portal, often found in public Wi-Fi networks where users need to log in or accept terms before accessing the internet.

Question 42:

In a console terminal, how can an ordinary user use the command nmcli to connect to the MyWifi wireless network protected by the password MyPassword? Options:

A) `nmcli connection add type wifi ssid MyWifi password MyPassword`

B) `nmcli device wifi connect MyWifi password MyPassword`

((Correct))

C) `nmcli device connect wifi MyWifi password MyPassword`

D) `nmcli connection up wifi MyWifi password MyPassword`

Explanation

The correct command syntax to connect to a Wi-Fi network

using `nmcli` is `nmcli device wifi connect SSID password PASSWORD`.

Question 43:

What command can turn the wireless adapter on if it was previously disabled by the operating system? Options:

A) `nmcli networking on`

B) `nmcli device wifi on`

C) `nmcli radio wifi on`

((Correct))

D) `nmcli connection up wifi`

Explanation

The command `nmcli radio wifi on` is used to turn the wireless adapter on if it was previously disabled by the operating system.

Question 44:

Custom configuration files should be placed in what directory when systemd-networkd is managing the network interfaces? Options:

A) `/etc/network/interfaces.d/`

B) `/etc/systemd/network/`

((Correct))

C) `/etc/netplan/`

D) `/etc/wpa_supplicant/`

Explanation

Custom configuration files for `systemd-networkd` should be placed in the directory `/etc/systemd/network/`.

Question 45:

How can a user run the command nmcli to delete an unused connection named HotelInternet? Options:

A) `nmcli connection delete HotelInternet`

((Correct))

B) `nmcli connection del HotelInternet`

C) `nmcli con delete HotelInternet`

D) `nmcli con del HotelInternet`

Explanation

The correct syntax to delete a connection using `nmcli` is `nmcli connection delete CONNECTION_NAME`.

Question 46:

Which test option in Bash scripting evaluates if a file is readable by the current user?

A) `-r`

((Correct))

B) `-w`

C) `-x`

D) `-e`

Explanation

The `-r` option evaluates if a file is readable by the current user in Bash scripting.

Question 47:

How could command test be used to verify if the file path stored in the variable FROM is newer than a file whose path is stored in the variable TO? Options:

A) `test "$FROM" -nt "$TO"`

((Correct))

B) `test "$FROM" -ot "$TO"`

C) `test "$TO" -nt "$FROM"`

D) `test "$TO" -ot "$FROM"`

Explanation

Option A correctly utilizes the `-nt` operator in the `test` command to check if the file path stored in the variable FROM is newer than the file whose path is stored in the variable TO.

Question 48:

The following script should print a number sequence from 0 to 9, but instead it indefinitely prints 0. What should be done to get the expected output?

#!/bin/bash

COUNTER=0

While [$COUNTER -lt 10]

do

echo $COUNTER

done

Options:

A) Add `let COUNTER++` inside the loop

B) Change `while [ $COUNTER -lt 10 ]` to `while [ $COUNTER -le 9 ]`

C) Initialize COUNTER as 1 instead of 0

D) Use `for COUNTER in {0..9}` instead of a while loop

A) Add `let COUNTER++` inside the loop

((Correct))

B) Change `while [ $COUNTER -lt 10 ]` to `while [ $COUNTER -le 9 ]`

C) Initialize COUNTER as 1 instead of 0

D) Use `for COUNTER in {0..9}` instead of a while loop

Explanation

Option A is the correct solution. Without an increment statement, the value of COUNTER remains 0, causing an infinite loop. Adding `let COUNTER++` inside the loop will increment the value of COUNTER in each iteration.

Question 49:

Suppose a user wrote a script that requires a sorted list of usernames. The resulting sorted list is presented as the following on his computer:

carol

Dave

emma

Frank

Grace

henry

However, the same list is sorted as the following on his colleague's computer:

Dave

Frank

Grace

carol

emma

henry

What could explain the differences between the two sorted lists?

Options:

A) Different locale settings

B) Different versions of the sort command

C) Different file permissions

D) Different file encoding

A) Different locale settings

((**Correct**))

B) Different versions of the sort command

C) Different file permissions

D) Different file encoding

Explanation

Option A is correct. Different locale settings, such as language and collation order, can affect how sorting is performed. Depending on the locale settings, the sorting order may vary, resulting in differences between sorted lists.

Question 50:

How could all of the script's command line arguments be used to initialize a Bash array? Options:

A) `args=("$@")`

((Correct))

B) `args=("$*")`

C) `args=($@)`

D) `args=($*)`

Explanation

Option A is correct. Using `"$@"` ensures that each command line argument is properly preserved, even if it contains spaces or special characters, and is assigned to the Bash array named args.

Question 51:

Why is it that, counter intuitively, the command test 1 > 2 evaluates as true? Options:

A) Because the '>' operator performs a greater-than

comparison

B) Because the '1' is considered larger than '2'

C) Because the redirection operator '>' redirects the output to a file named '2'

((Correct))

D) Because '2' evaluates as false

Explanation

Option C is correct. In Bash, the '>' operator is used for redirection, so `test 1 > 2` redirects the output of the command `test 1` to a file named '2', and the command returns true if the file '2' is created successfully.

Question 52:

What command would you use to determine what Xorg extensions are available on a system? Options:

A) `ls /usr/lib/xorg/modules/extensions`

B) `xwininfo`

C) `xdpyinfo`

((Correct))

D) `xev`

Explanation

Option C is correct. The `xdpyinfo` command provides information about the X server, including the available Xorg extensions.

Question 53:

You have just received a brand new 10-button mouse for your computer, however, it will require extra configuration in order to get all of the buttons to function properly. Without modifying the rest of the X server configuration, what directory would you use to create a new configuration file for this mouse, and what specific configuration section would be used in this file? Options:

A) Directory: ` /etc/X11/xorg.conf.d/ `; Section: ` InputClass `

((**Correct**))

B) Directory: ` /usr/share/X11/xorg.conf.d/ `; Section: ` ServerLayout `

C) Directory: ` /etc/X11/ `; Section: ` InputDevice `

D) Directory: ` /usr/lib/X11/ `; Section: ` Device `

Explanation

Option A is correct. The directory ` /etc/X11/xorg.conf.d/ ` is commonly used to store configuration files for specific devices or input classes, and the ` InputClass ` section is appropriate for configuring input devices like mice.

Question 54:

What component of a Linux installation is responsible for keeping an X server running? Options:

A) Xinit

B) X Window System

C) Display Manager

((**Correct**))

D) Window Manager

Explanation

Option C is correct. The Display Manager, such as `lightdm` or `gdm`, is responsible for starting and managing the X server during system boot.

Question 55:

Which remote desktop protocol provides native features to integrate local and remote systems, such as accessing local devices from the remote machine?

A) VNC

B) RDP

C) XDMCP

D) Spice

((Correct))

Explanation

Spice comprises a suite of tools aimed at accessing the desktop environment of virtualized systems, offering native features to integrate local and remote systems, such as accessing local devices from the remote machine and file sharing between the two systems.

Question 56:

Which desktop environment is often the first choice in distributions like Fedora, Debian, and Ubuntu?

A) KDE

B) Gnome

((Correct))

C) Xfce

D) LXDE

Explanation

Gnome is often the first choice in distributions like Fedora, Debian, and Ubuntu. It introduced major changes in its look and structure with version 3, including the introduction of Gnome Shell.

Question 57:

What is the purpose of a desktop entry in a Linux desktop environment?

A) To store user passwords securely

B) To define the appearance of desktop icons

C) To provide information about available desktop applications and how to use them

((Correct))

D) To manage the desktop background image

Explanation

Desktop entries are text files used by the desktop environment to gather information about available desktop applications and how to use them.

Question 58:

How could the Bounce keys accessibility feature help users whose involuntary hand tremors disturb their typing?

Options:

A) By repeating a keystroke if it is held down for a certain period

B) By slowing down the keyboard repeat rate

C) By delaying keystrokes to filter out unintentional multiple key presses

((Correct))

D) By activating a key after it has been pressed twice in quick succession

Explanation

Option C is correct. Bounce keys delay keystrokes to filter out unintentional multiple key presses, which can help users with hand tremors type more accurately.

Question 59:

What is the most common Activation Gesture for the Sticky keys accessibility feature? Options:

A) Double tap

B) Triple tap

C) Long press

D) Single tap

((Correct))

Explanation

Option D is correct. The most common Activation Gesture for Sticky keys is a single tap of the Shift, Ctrl, Alt, or Windows key, which allows users to activate the feature without needing to press multiple keys simultaneously.

Question 60:

Accessibility features may not be provided by a single application and may vary from one desktop environment to another. In KDE, what application helps those with repetitive strain injuries by clicking the mouse whenever the mouse cursor pauses briefly? Options:

A) MouseTweaks

((Correct))

B) Onboard

C) Orca

D) Screen reader

Explanation

Option A is correct. In KDE, MouseTweaks is the application that helps users with repetitive strain injuries by clicking the mouse whenever the mouse cursor pauses briefly.

Question 61:

Observe the following output and answer the following questions:

cat /etc/passwd | grep '\(root\|mail\|catherine\|kevin\)'

root:x:0:0:root:/root:/bin/bash

mail:x:8:8:mail:/var/spool/mail:/sbin/nologin

catherine:x:1030:1025:User   Chaterine:/home/catherine:/bin/bash kevin:x:1040:1015:User Kevin:/home/kevin:/bin/bash

Identify the User IDs (UIDs) and Group IDs (GIDs) for the root and catherine users:

Options:

A) UID: 0, GID: 0; UID: 1030, GID: 1025

B) UID: 0, GID: 0; UID: 1040, GID: 1015

C) UID: 0, GID: 0; UID: 1030, GID: 1015

D) UID: 1040, GID: 1015; UID: 1030, GID: 1025

A) UID: 0, GID: 0; UID: 1030, GID: 1025

((Correct))

B) UID: 0, GID: 0; UID: 1040, GID: 1015

C) UID: 0, GID: 0; UID: 1030, GID: 1015

D) UID: 1040, GID: 1015; UID: 1030, GID: 1025

Explanation

Option A correctly identifies the User IDs (UIDs) and Group IDs (GIDs) for the root and catherine users.

Question 62:

By convention, which IDs are assigned to system accounts and which to ordinary users? Options:

A) System accounts have UIDs below 1000, while ordinary users have UIDs above 1000.

((Correct))

B) System accounts have GIDs below 1000, while ordinary

users have GIDs above 1000.

C) System accounts have UIDs above 1000, while ordinary users have UIDs below 1000.

D) System accounts have GIDs above 1000, while ordinary users have GIDs below 1000.

Explanation

Option A accurately describes the convention where system accounts typically have lower User IDs (UIDs) while ordinary user accounts have higher UIDs.

Question 63:

How do you find out if a user account, which was previously able to access the system, is now locked? Assume your system uses shadow passwords. Options:

A) Check the /etc/passwd file for an exclamation mark (!) at the beginning of the password field.

B) Check the /etc/shadow file for an exclamation mark (!) at the beginning of the password field.

((Correct))

C) Use the passwd -S command to check the status of the user account.

D) Use the chage -l command to check the password aging information of the user account.

Explanation

Option B is correct as in the /etc/shadow file, an exclamation mark (!) at the beginning of the password field indicates a locked account.

Question 64:

Create a user account named christian using the useradd -m command and identify its UserID (UID), Group ID (GID), and shell. Options:

A) The UID is assigned automatically, the GID is 1000, and the shell is /bin/bash.

((Correct))

B) The UID is assigned automatically, the GID is 1001, and the shell is /bin/bash.

C) The UID is assigned automatically, the GID is 1000, and the shell is /bin/sh.

D) The UID is assigned automatically, the GID is 1001, and the shell is /bin/sh.

Explanation

Option A is correct as the useradd -m command automatically assigns a UID, sets the GID to 1000 (typically the primary users group), and assigns the default shell as /bin/bash.

Question 65:

Identify the name of the primary group of christian. What can you deduce? Options:

A) christian

((Correct))

B) users

C) christian

D) users

Explanation

Option A correctly identifies the primary group of the user christian, which typically has the same name as the username by convention.

Question 66:

Using the getent command, review password aging information for the christian user account. Options:

A) getent passwd christian

B) getent shadow christian

((Correct))

C) chage -l christian

D) passwd -S christian

Explanation

Option B is correct as the getent command is used to query entries in databases configured in /etc/nsswitch.conf, and shadow is the database for password aging information.

Question 67:

Once you have scheduled a job with `at`, how can you review its commands? Options:

A) `atq`

((Correct))

B) `at -l`

C) `at -v`

D) `at -c`

Explanation

Option A (`atq`) is used to list the user's pending `at` jobs.

Question 68:

Which commands can you use to review your pending `at` jobs? Which commands would you use to delete them? Options:

A) `atq` to review and `atrm` to delete.

((Correct))

B) `at -l` to review and `at -r` to delete.

C) `at -v` to review and `at -d` to delete.

D) `at -c` to review and `at -x` to delete.

Explanation

Option A is correct. `atq` lists the pending jobs, and `atrm` removes them.

Question 69:

With systemd, which command is used as an alternative to `at`? Options:

A) `timed`

B) `timerctl`

C) `systemctl`

((Correct))

D) `timedatectl`

Explanation

Option C is correct. `systemctl` provides an alternative to `at` for scheduling tasks with systemd.

Question 70:

Create an at job that runs the foo.sh script, located in your home directory, at 10:30 AM on coming October 31st. Assume you are acting as an ordinary user.

A) echo "/path/to/foo.sh" | at 10:30 AM October 31

((Correct))

B) cat "/path/to/foo.sh" | at 10:30 AM October 31

C) grep "/path/to/foo.sh" | at 10:30 AM October 31

D) list "/path/to/foo.sh" | at 10:30 AM October 31

Explanation

The correct answer is **A)** echo "/path/to/foo.sh" | at 10:30 AM October 31.

A) echo "/path/to/foo.sh" | at 10:30 AM October 31: This command pipes the path to the foo.sh script to the at command, scheduling it to run at the specified time and date.

B) cat "/path/to/foo.sh" | at 10:30 AM October 31: This command uses cat to display the content of the script and pipes it to the at command, which is not the correct way to schedule an at job.

C) grep "/path/to/foo.sh" | at 10:30 AM October 31: This command uses grep to search for the script's path, then pipes the output to the at command, which is incorrect for scheduling an at job.

D) list "/path/to/foo.sh" | at 10:30 AM October 31: There is no list command in Linux for scheduling at jobs. This is an incorrect command.

Detailed Explanation:

The at command is used to schedule commands or scripts to be executed at a later time. To schedule the execution of a script, you typically use echo to specify the command to be executed and pipe it to the at command.

In this case, the correct command is:

$ echo "/path/to/foo.sh" | at 10:30 AM October 31

Here, echo is used to print the path to the script, and the output is piped to the at command. The at command reads the command from the standard input and schedules it to run at 10:30 AM on October 31st.

Understanding how to use the at command is essential for scheduling one-time tasks or scripts to run at specific times in Linux systems. It provides a convenient way to automate tasks without the need for complex scheduling tools or services.

Question 71:

NetworkManager scans wi-fi networks periodically and command nmcli device wifi list only lists the access points found in the last scan. How should the nmcli command be used to ask NetworkManager to immediately re-scan all available access points? Options:

A) `nmcli device wifi rescan`

B) `nmcli device wifi refresh`

C) `nmcli device wifi scan`

((Correct))

D) `nmcli device wifi reload`

Explanation

The command `nmcli device wifi scan` instructs NetworkManager to immediately re-scan all available access points.

Question 72:

What name entry should be used in the [Match] section of a systemd-networkd configuration file to match all ethernet interfaces? Options:

A) `Type=ethernet`

B) `Name=*`

C) `Name=eth*`

((Correct))

D) `Type=ether`

Explanation

The entry `Name=eth*` in the [Match] section of a systemd-networkd configuration file matches all ethernet interfaces whose names start with "eth".

Question 73:

How should the wpa_passphrase command be executed to use the passphrase given as an argument and not from the standard input? Options:

A) `wpa_passphrase SSID passphrase`

B) `wpa_passphrase SSID < passphrase`

C) `echo passphrase | wpa_passphrase SSID`

D) `wpa_passphrase SSID <<< passphrase`

((Correct))

Explanation

The syntax `wpa_passphrase SSID <<< passphrase` allows using the passphrase provided as an argument and not from the standard input.

Question 74:

What command would show you if any processes are listening on TCP port 80?

A) `netstat -tuln`

B) `lsof -i :80`

C) `ss -tulw`

D) All of the above

((Correct))

Explanation

All of the listed commands (`netstat -tuln`, `lsof -i :80`, `ss -tulw`) can be used to show processes listening on TCP port 80.

Question 75:

How could you find which process is listening on a port?

A) `ps aux | grep PORT`

B) `lsof -i :PORT`

((**Correct**))

C) `netstat -tuln`

D) All of the above

Explanation

The `lsof` command with the `-i` option followed by the port number can be used to find which process is listening on a specific port.

Question 76:

How could you determine the max MTU of a network path?

A) `traceroute -m`

B) `ping -M do -s MTU HOST`

((**Correct**))

C) `netstat -i`

D) `ip route get HOST`

Explanation

By using the `ping` command with the `-M do` option and specifying the desired MTU size with the `-s` option, you can determine the maximum MTU of a network path.

Question 77:

How could you use netcat to send an HTTP request to a web server?

A) `nc -l 80`

B) `nc -u 80`

C) `nc -w3 google.com 80`

D) `echo -e "GET / HTTP/1.1\r\nHost: google.com\r\n\r\n" | nc google.com 80`

((**Correct**))

Explanation

This command sends an HTTP GET request to `google.com` on port 80 using netcat.

Question 78:

What are a few reasons pinging a host can fail?

A) Firewall blocking ICMP traffic, host offline, incorrect IP address

((**Correct**))

B) DNS resolution failure, incorrect subnet mask, network congestion

C) Incorrect routing table, DNS cache corruption, MTU mismatch

D) All of the above

Explanation

These are common reasons why pinging a host can fail.

Question 79:

Name a tool you could use to see network packets reaching or leaving a Linux host?

A) tcpdump

((**Correct**))

B) netstat

C) traceroute

D) nslookup

Explanation

tcpdump is a tool used to capture and analyze network packets.

Question 80:

What is the purpose of the host command in Linux?

A) To display entries from name service databases

B) To query DNS servers for DNS entries

((**Correct**))

C) To configure local name resolution

D) To set resolver options

Explanation

The host command is used to query DNS servers for DNS entries in Linux.

Question 81:

Which command is more suited for troubleshooting DNS server configuration in Linux?

A) getent

B) host

C) dig

((**Correct**))

D) nslookup

Explanation

The dig command provides verbose output and is more suited for troubleshooting DNS server configuration in Linux.

Question 82:

What will the command ` getent group openldap` do?

A) Display information about the openldap group.

B) Retrieve the entry for the openldap group from the /etc/ group file.

C) Retrieve information about users belonging to the openldap group from the system's group database.

((**Correct**))

D) Check if the openldap group exists on the system.

Explanation

The `getent group openldap` command retrieves information about the openldap group from the system's group database.

Question 83:

What is the biggest difference between `getent` and the other tools covered, `host` and `dig`?

A) `getent` retrieves information from the system's databases while `host` and `dig` perform DNS queries.

((Correct))

B) `getent` is used for querying network information while `host` and `dig` are used for retrieving DNS records.

C) `getent` is specific to querying user and group information while `host` and `dig` are used for DNS queries.

D) There is no significant difference between `getent` and `host`/`dig`.

Explanation

`getent` is used to retrieve entries from the system's databases like `/etc/passwd`, `/etc/group`, etc., while `host` and `dig` are specifically used for DNS queries.

Question 84:

Which option to `dig` and `host` is used to specify the type of record you wish to retrieve?

A) -t

((Correct))

B) -r

C) -q

D) -s

Explanation

The `-t` option in both `dig` and `host` is used to specify the type of DNS record you want to retrieve.

Question 85:

How can the previously locked account emma be unlocked?

A) Using the `unlock` command followed by the username.

B) Editing the /etc/passwd file and changing the locked field to '0'.

C) Running the `passwd -u emma` command.

((Correct))

D) Deleting the /etc/nologin file.

Explanation

The `passwd -u` command is used to unlock a user account.

Question 86:

How can the expiration date of the account emma get set to never?

A) By editing the /etc/shadow file and removing the expiration date field.

B) Using the `chage -E -1 emma` command.

((Correct))

C) Running the `passwd -n -1 emma` command.

D) Setting the expiration date to '99999' in the /etc/passwd file.

Explanation

The `chage -E -1` command sets the expiration date to never for the specified user.

Question 87:

Imagine the CUPS printing service handling print jobs is not needed on your server. How can you disable the service permanently? How can you check the appropriate port is not active anymore?

A) Use the `systemctl disable cups` command and then check with `netstat -tuln` for port 631.

B) Use the `systemctl stop cups` command and then check with `lsof -i :631`.

C) Use the `systemctl mask cups` command and then check with `ss -tuln`.

((Correct))

D) Use the `service cups stop` command and then check with `nmap localhost`.

Explanation

The `systemctl mask` command not only stops the service but also prevents it from being started again, even manually. Checking with `ss -tuln` will show if port 631, used by CUPS, is active.

Question 88:

What is the purpose of a revocation certificate in GPG?

A) To revoke the public key

((Correct))

B) To revoke the private key

C) To revoke the trust database

D) To revoke the key pair

Explanation

A revocation certificate is used to revoke a public key in case it is compromised or no longer needed.

Question 89:

How can a user export their public key in GPG for distribution to others?

A) gpg --export-public-key

B) gpg --send-keys

C) gpg --export

((Correct))

D) gpg --share-key

Explanation

The command `gpg --export` is used to export the public key for distribution to others.

Question 90:

What is the purpose of ASCII armored output in GPG?

A) To compress the encrypted data

B) To increase the security of encryption

C) To generate a human-readable format for distribution

((Correct))

D) To improve decryption performance

Explanation

ASCII armored output converts the binary encrypted data into a human-readable format, which is useful for distribution via email or other text-based methods.

PRACTICE TEST SIX - LPIC-1 EXAM 102 VERSION: 5.0

90 questions | 2 hours | 90% correct required to pass

The LPIC-1 Exam 102 Version: 5.0 Practice Test is a comprehensive resource designed to prepare you for the LPIC-1 (Linux Professional Institute Certification) Exam 102. It includes practice questions that mimic the format and content of the actual test. Each **Question** comes with a detailed **Explanation** to help you understand the concepts better. This practice test is an excellent tool to harness the power of Linux and achieve LPIC-1 certification.

Question 1:

As an ordinary user, log in to the system and create an at job that runs the foobar.sh script just after 30 minutes. Assume the script is located in the user's home directory.

A) echo "~/foobar.sh" | at now + 30 minutes

(((**Correct**)))

B) echo "~/foobar.sh" | at 30 minutes

C) echo "sh ~/foobar.sh" | at now + 30 minutes

D) echo "bash ~/foobar.sh" | at 30 minutes

Explanation

The correct answer is:

A) echo "~/foobar.sh" | at now + 30 minutes

This command correctly creates an at job to run the foobar.sh script located in the user's home directory just after 30 minutes. Here's the breakdown of the command:

echo "~/foobar.sh": This echoes the path to the script foobar.sh, assuming it is located in the user's home directory (~ represents the home directory).

| at now + 30 minutes: This pipes the echoed path to the at command, scheduling the script to run after 30 minutes from the current time.

Option B is incorrect because it does not specify the time relative to the current time, which is necessary for scheduling the job correctly.

Option C is incorrect because it explicitly specifies sh to execute the script, which is unnecessary and may lead to unexpected behavior.

Option D is incorrect because it explicitly specifies bash to execute the script, which is unnecessary and may lead to unexpected behavior.

Understanding how to use the at command is essential for scheduling tasks to run at specific times in Linux systems. Proper usage ensures efficient task management and automation.

Question 2:

As root, run the `atq` command to review the scheduled `at` jobs of all users. What happens if an ordinary user executes this command? Options:

A) Ordinary users can view their own `at` jobs.

((Correct))

B) Ordinary users can view all `at` jobs on the system.

C) Ordinary users cannot view any `at` jobs.

D) Ordinary users can view only root's `at` jobs.

Explanation

Option A is correct. Ordinary users can only view their own `at` jobs, not those of other users.

Question 3:

As root, delete all these pending `at` jobs using a single command. Options:

A) `at -l | awk '{print $1}' | xargs atrm`

B) `atq | awk '{print $1}' | xargs atrm`

((Correct))

C) `atrm -a`

D) `atq | atrm`

Explanation

Option B correctly lists the `at` jobs and removes them using `atrm`.

Question 4:

Run the `ls -l /usr/bin/at` command and examine its permissions. Options:

A) `-rwxr-xr-x`

B) `-rwsr-sr-x`

((Correct))

C) `-rwsr-xr-x`

D) `-r-xr-xr-x`

Explanation

Option B is correct. The `s` in the owner and group execute permission bits indicates that the `at` command has the setuid and setgid bits set, allowing users to run it with the permissions of the file owner and group.

Question 5:

What command will make Pacific/Auckland the default time zone for the current shell session? Options:

A) `export TZ=Pacific/Auckland`

((Correct))

B) `setenv TZ Pacific/Auckland`

C) `TZ=Pacific/Auckland`

D) `set TZ=Pacific/Auckland`

Explanation

Option A correctly sets the `TZ` environment variable to `Pacific/Auckland` for the current shell session.

Question 6:

Command `uptime` shows, among other things, the load average of the system in fractional numbers. It uses the current locale settings to decide if the decimal place separator should be a dot or a comma. What command will make `uptime` display the fractions using a dot instead of a comma for the rest of the current session? Options:

A) `export LC_NUMERIC=en_US.UTF-8`

((Correct))

B) `setenv LC_NUMERIC en_US.UTF-8`

C) `LC_NUMERIC=en_US.UTF-8`

D) `set LC_NUMERIC=en_US.UTF-8`

Explanation

Option A sets the `LC_NUMERIC` environment variable to `en_US.UTF-8`, ensuring that `uptime` uses a dot as the decimal separator.

Question 7:

Command `iconv` will replace all characters outside the target character set with a question mark. If `//TRANSLIT` is appended to the target encoding, characters not represented in the target character set will be replaced (transliterated) by one or more similar looking characters. How could this method be used to convert a UTF-8 text file named `readme.txt` to a plain ASCII file named `ascii.txt`? Options:

A) `iconv -f UTF-8 -t ASCII//TRANSLIT readme.txt > ascii.txt`

((**Correct**))

B) `iconv -f ASCII//TRANSLIT -t UTF-8 readme.txt > ascii.txt`

C) `iconv -f UTF-8 -t ASCII readme.txt > ascii.txt`

D) `iconv -f ASCII -t UTF-8//TRANSLIT readme.txt > ascii.txt`

Explanation

Option A correctly specifies the source encoding `-f UTF-8`, the target encoding `-t ASCII//TRANSLIT`, and the input file `readme.txt`, with output redirection to `ascii.txt`.

Question 8:

Command `uptime` shows, among other things, the load average of the system in fractional numbers. It uses the current locale settings to decide if the decimal place separator should be a dot or a comma. What command will make `uptime` display the fractions using a dot instead of a comma for the rest of the current session? Options:

A) `export LC_NUMERIC=en_US.UTF-8`

((**Correct**))

B) `setenv LC_NUMERIC en_US.UTF-8`

C) `LC_NUMERIC=en_US.UTF-8`

D) `set LC_NUMERIC=en_US.UTF-8`

Explanation

Option A sets the `LC_NUMERIC` environment variable to `en_US.UTF-8`, ensuring that `uptime` uses a dot as the decimal separator.

Question 9:

Command `iconv` will replace all characters outside the target character set with a question mark. If `//TRANSLIT` is appended to the target encoding, characters not represented in the target character set will be replaced (transliterated) by one or more similar looking characters. How could this method be used to convert a UTF-8 text file named `readme.txt` to a plain ASCII file named `ascii.txt`? Options:

A) `iconv -f UTF-8 -t ASCII//TRANSLIT readme.txt > ascii.txt`

((Correct))

B) `iconv -f ASCII//TRANSLIT -t UTF-8 readme.txt > ascii.txt`

C) `iconv -f UTF-8 -t ASCII readme.txt > ascii.txt`

D) `iconv -f ASCII -t UTF-8//TRANSLIT readme.txt > ascii.txt`

Explanation

Option A correctly specifies the source encoding `-f UTF-8`, the target encoding `-t ASCII//TRANSLIT`, and the input file `readme.txt`, with output redirection to `ascii.txt`.

Question 10:

Research the differences between SNTP and NTP.

Options:

A) SNTP provides more accurate time synchronization.

B) SNTP is a simplified version of NTP.

C) NTP includes authentication mechanisms, while SNTP does not.

((Correct))

D) SNTP is suitable for critical time synchronization tasks.

Explanation

- SNTP (Simple Network Time Protocol) is indeed a simplified version of NTP.

- NTP (Network Time Protocol) provides greater accuracy and includes authentication mechanisms.

Question 11:

Why might a system administrator choose not to use pool.ntp.org? Options:

A) Concerns about reliance on external servers.

B) Security concerns regarding trustworthiness of servers.

C) Preference for using internal time servers.

D) All of the above.

((Correct))

Explanation

All the listed reasons are valid concerns that may lead a system administrator to choose not to use pool.ntp.org.

Question 12:

How would a system administrator choose to join or otherwise contribute to the pool.ntp.org project? Options:

A) Register the server with pool.ntp.org.

B) Configure the server to act as a public NTP server.

C) Monitor and maintain the server for accurate time synchronization.

D) All of the above.

((Correct))

Explanation

Registering the server, configuring it as a public NTP server, and maintaining it are all ways a system administrator can contribute to the pool.ntp.org project.

Question 13:

Assuming you are root, check if the following journalctl command table is correct.

Purpose: Command

Print kernel entries: *journalctl -k*

Print messages from the second boot starting at beginning of journal: *journalctl -b -2*

Print messages from the second boot starting at end of journal: *journalctl -b -2 -r*

Print most recent log messages and keep watching for new ones: *journalctl -f*

Print only new messages since now, and update the output continuously: *journalctl -f --since=now*

Print messages from the previous boot with a priority of

warning and in reverse order: *journalctl -b -1 -p warning -r*

A) (Correct)

((Correct))

B) Not correct

Explanation

These commands provide various functionalities for viewing logs using journalctl, a utility for querying and displaying logs from the systemd journal:

1. Print kernel entries: journalctl -k

2. Print messages from the second boot starting at the beginning of the journal: journalctl -b -2

3. Print messages from the second boot starting at the end of the journal: journalctl -b -2 -r

4. Print most recent log messages and keep watching for new ones: journalctl -f

5. Print only new messages since now, and update the output continuously: journalctl -f --since=now

6. Print messages from the previous boot with a priority of warning and in reverse order: journalctl -b -1 -p warning -r
> -b -1: This specifies that you want to view logs from the last boot (-b) and specifically from the most recent one (-1).
> -p warning: This filters the output to only show messages with a priority level of "warning". Possible priority levels include emerg, alert, crit, error, warning, notice, info, and debug.
> -r: This sorts the output in reverse chronological order, with the most recent messages appearing first.

Question 14:

Check if the behaviors are related to values in the following lines:

- For **Storage=auto**, log data is thrown away but forwarding is possible.

- For **Storage=none**, log data will be stored under /var/log/journal if not already present, creating the directory.

- For **Storage=persistent**, log data will be stored under /var/log/journal if not already present, but the directory won't be created.

- For **Storage=volatile**, log data will be stored under /var/run/journal but won't survive reboots.

A) True

((**Correct**))

B) False

Explanation

The correct answer is: True

- For **Storage=auto**: Log data is stored in volatile memory but is thrown away when memory is full. However, forwarding to a centralized logging system is possible.

- For **Storage=none**: Log data is stored on disk under /var/log/journal if the directory doesn't exist, and the directory is created if necessary.

- For **Storage=persistent**: Log data is stored on disk under /var/log/journal if the directory doesn't exist. However, the directory won't be created if it doesn't exist.

- For **Storage=volatile**: Log data is stored in volatile memory under /var/run/journal and won't survive reboots.

Understanding the behavior of the Storage option in /etc/systemd/journald.conf is essential for managing systemd journaling in Linux systems. Different storage options offer varying levels of persistence and flexibility in handling log data, catering to different system requirements and use cases.

Question 15:

As you learned, the journal can be manually vacuumed based on time, size, and number of files. Check if the following journalctl commands are correct:

1. Check how much disk space is taken up by journal files:

journalctl --disk-usage

2. Cut down on the quantity of space reserved for archived journal files and set it to 200MiB:

journalctl --vacuum-size=200M

3. Check on disk space again and explain the results:

journalctl --disk-usage

A) (Correct)

((Correct))

B) Not correct

Explanation

These commands allow for managing disk space occupied

by journal files, including checking current usage, adjusting reserved space, and verifying the changes.

Question 16:

What is the primary role of Mail User Agents (MUAs) in email communication?

A) Routing email messages between MTAs

B) Storing email messages in the user's mailbox

C) Composing, reading, and managing email messages

((Correct))

D) Providing network connectivity for email communication

Explanation

MUAs are email client applications that allow users to compose, send, receive, read, and manage email messages.

Question 17:

Which command is used to enter send mode in the `mail` command in a Unix-like operating system?

A) mail

B) mailq

C) mail -s

D) mail recipient@example.com

((Correct))

Explanation

Providing an email address as an argument to the `mail`

command enters send mode, allowing users to compose and send email messages directly from the command line.

Question 18:

Study the columns "Alias Name" and "Aliased Command(s)" and check if all the aliases are assigned to their values correctly:

| Alias Name | Aliased Command(s) | Alias Assignment |

| b | `bash` | **alias b=bash** |

| bash_info | `which bash + echo "$BASH_VERSION"` | **alias bash_info='which bash; echo "$BASH_VERSION"'** |

| kernel_info | `uname -r` | **alias kernel_info='uname -r'** |

| greet | `echo Hi, $USER!` | **alias greet='echo Hi, $USER'** |

| computer | `pc=slimbook + echo My computer is a $pc` | **alias computer='pc=slimbook; echo My computer is a $pc'** |

A) Yes

((Correct))

B) No

Explanation

1. b is correctly assigned to `bash`, creating a shorthand for invoking the Bash shell.
2. bash_info is correctly assigned.
3. kernel_info is correctly assigned to `uname -r`, providing kernel information.
4. greet is correctly assigned to `echo Hi, $USER!`, generating a personalized greeting.
5. computer is correctly assigned.

Question 19:

Which command correctly makes a function read-only, and how do you list all read-only functions?

A) readonly -f my_fun

((**Correct**))

B) readonly my_fun

C) readonly -f my_fun

D) readonly -f my_fun && declare -f | grep 'readonly'

Explanation

The correct answer is:

A) readonly -f my_fun

To make a function read-only, you use the readonly command with the -f option followed by the function name. For example, readonly -f my_fun makes the function my_fun read-only, preventing any modifications to its definition.

The incorrect options and their explanations:

B) readonly my_fun: This command makes a variable read-only, not a function.

C) readonly -f my_fun: This command syntax is incorrect. If you use -f with readonly, it should directly follow the command without any space in between.

D) readonly -f my_fun && declare -f | grep 'readonly': While the first part (readonly -f my_fun) correctly makes the function my_fun read-only, the second part (declare -f | grep 'readonly') lists all function definitions and filters out read-only functions. However, combining these commands with && would execute them sequentially, and the second command will execute regardless of whether the first command succeeded or not, which is unnecessary.

Therefore, option A is the correct choice for making a function read-only.

Understanding how to make functions read-only is crucial for protecting critical functions from unintended modifications, and ensuring the integrity of the codebase. Additionally, knowing how to list read-only functions provides a useful tool for managing and maintaining code in shell scripting environments.

Question 20:

The following task involves modifying the PS1 variable, which controls the prompt format in Bash, and creating a function that echoes various system information. Check if the function `fyi` is implemented correctly:

fyi() {

echo "User: $USER"

echo "Home directory: $HOME"

echo "Host: $HOSTNAME"

echo "Operating system: $(uname -s)"

echo "Search path for executables: $PATH"

echo "Mail directory: $MAIL"

*echo "Mail check interval: $(grep -i '^[[:space:]]*MAILCHECK' / etc/profile)"*

echo "Shell depth: $SHLVL"

```
}
```

```
# Modify PS1 to show <user>@<host-date>
PS1="\[\e[1;32m\]\u@\h-\d\[\e[0m\]:\w\$ "
```

A) True

((Correct))

B) False

Explanation

This function can be added to a startup script like `.bashrc` or `.bash_profile` to provide the user with the specified system information and modify the prompt accordingly. The PS1 modification ensures that the prompt displays the username followed by the hostname and date.

Question 21:

How would a user temporarily change the default field separator to the newline character only, while still being able to revert it to its original content? Options:

A) `IFS=$'\n'` to change, `unset IFS` to revert

((Correct))

B) `IFS='\n'` to change, `IFS=''` to revert

C) `IFS=$'\n'` to change, `IFS='\t'` to revert

D) `IFS='\n'` to change, `unset IFS` to revert

Explanation

Option A is correct. To temporarily change the default field separator to the newline character, `IFS` can be set to `` `$'\n'` ``, and to revert it to its original content, `IFS` can be unset (`unset IFS`).

Question 22:

What command line switch is used with the X command to create a new xorg.conf configuration file? Options:

A) `-configure`

((Correct))

B) `-createconfig`

C) `-newconfig`

D) `-xorgconf`

Explanation

Option A is correct. The `-configure` switch with the `X` command is used to automatically generate a new `xorg.conf` configuration file based on the current hardware configuration.

Question 23:

What would the contents of the DISPLAY environment variable be on a system named lab01 using a single display configuration? Assume that the DISPLAY environment variable is being viewed in a terminal emulator on the third independent screen. Options:

A) `:0.2`

((Correct))

B) `lab01:0.2`

C) `:3`

D) `lab01:3`

Explanation

Option A is correct. In a single display configuration, the DISPLAY environment variable typically follows the format `:<display_number>.<screen_number>`, so on the third independent screen, the screen number would be 2, resulting in `:0.2`.

Question 24:

What command can be used to create a keyboard configuration file for use by the X Window System? Options:

A) `xset`

B) `setxkbmap`

C) `xmodmap`

D) `xkbcomp`

((Correct))

Explanation

Option D is correct. The `xkbcomp` command is used to compile XKB (X Keyboard Extension) descriptions into keymap files, which can then be used as keyboard configuration files by the X Window System.

Question 25:

On a typical Linux installation, a user can switch to a virtual terminal by pressing the Ctrl + Alt + F1 - F6 keys on a keyboard. You have been asked to set up a kiosk system with

LPIC-1 102-500 V5 EXAM PREP: MASTER LINUX ADMIN WITH 6 PRACTIC...

a graphical interface and need this feature disabled to prevent unauthorized tampering with the system. You decide to create a /etc/X11/xorg.conf.d/10-kiosk.conf configuration file. Using a ServerFlags section (which is used to set global Xorg options on the server), what option would need to be specified? Review the xorg(1) man page to locate the option. Options:

A) `DontVTSwitch`

((Correct))

B) `VTSwitch`

C) `NoVTSwitch`

D) `DisableVTSwitch`

Explanation

Option A is correct. The `DontVTSwitch` option, when set to `true` in the ServerFlags section of an Xorg configuration file, prevents users from switching to virtual terminals using Ctrl + Alt + F1 - F6 keys.

Question 26:

Which remote desktop protocol is platform-independent and uses the Remote Frame Buffer protocol (RFB)?

A) VNC

((Correct))

B) RDP

C) XDMCP

D) Spice

Explanation

2

Virtual Network Computing (VNC) is platform-independent and uses the Remote Frame Buffer protocol (RFB) to view and control remote desktop environments.

Question 27:

Which component of a desktop environment is responsible for listing built-in and third-party applications available in the system?

A) Window manager

B) File manager

C) Application launcher

((Correct))

D) Taskbar

Explanation

The application launcher is responsible for listing built-in and third-party applications available in the system, providing users with a convenient way to access them.

Question 28:

What type of application provides windowed shell sessions in the desktop environment? Options:

A) Terminal emulator

((Correct))

B) File manager

C) Web browser

D) Text editor

Explanation

Option A is correct. A terminal emulator provides windowed shell sessions in the desktop environment, allowing users to interact with the command line interface within a graphical window.

Question 29:

Due to the variety of Linux desktop environments, the same application may have more than one version, each of them best suited for a particular widget toolkit. For example, the bittorrent client Transmission has two versions: transmission-gtk and transmission-qt. Which of the two should be installed to ensure maximum integration with KDE? Options:

A) transmission-gtk

B) transmission-qt

((Correct))

C) transmission-cli

D) transmission-core

Explanation

Option B is correct. KDE uses the Qt widget toolkit, so installing the `transmission-qt` version ensures maximum integration with KDE.

Question 30:

What Linux desktop environments are recommended for low-cost single board computers with little processing power? Options:

A) GNOME and KDE

B) Xfce and LXQt

((Correct))

C) Cinnamon and MATE

D) Unity and Pantheon

Explanation

Option B is correct. Xfce and LXQt are lightweight desktop environments designed to run efficiently on low-cost single board computers with limited processing power.

Question 31:

There are two ways to copy and paste text in the X Window System: using the traditional Ctrl + c and Ctrl + v keystrokes (also available in the window menu) or to use the mouse middle-button click to paste the currently selected text. What's the appropriate way to copy and paste text from a terminal emulator? Options:

A) Ctrl + c and Ctrl + v

((Correct))

B) Mouse middle-button click

C) Right-click and select "Copy" and "Paste"

D) Ctrl + x and Ctrl + p

Explanation

Option A is correct. In a terminal emulator, the appropriate way to copy and paste text is to use the Ctrl + c and Ctrl + v keyboard shortcuts.

Question 32:

Most desktop environments assign the Alt + F2 keyboard shortcut to the Run program window, where programs can be executed in a command line fashion. In KDE, what command would execute the default terminal emulator? Options:

A) `konsole`

((Correct))

B) `gnome-terminal`

C) `xterm`

D) `terminator`

Explanation

Option A is correct. In KDE, the default terminal emulator is `konsole`, so executing the `konsole` command would open the default terminal emulator using the Alt + F2 shortcut.

Question 33:

What protocol is best suited to access a remote Windows desktop from a Linux desktop environment? Options:

A) SSH (Secure Shell)

B) RDP (Remote Desktop Protocol)

((Correct))

C) VNC (Virtual Network Computing)

D) FTP (File Transfer Protocol)

Explanation

Option B is correct. RDP (Remote Desktop Protocol) is best suited to access a remote Windows desktop from a Linux desktop environment.

Question 34:

What appearance aspects of the graphical environment can be modified to make it easier for people to read text on the screen? Options:

A) Font size and color contrast

((Correct))

B) Screen resolution and refresh rate

C) Desktop background and icon size

D) Window transparency and animation effects

Explanation

Option A is correct. Modifying font size and color contrast can make text easier to read on the screen for people with visual impairments.

Question 35:

In what ways can the Orca application help visually impaired users to interact with the desktop environment? Options:

A) By providing voice feedback for screen content and keyboard input

((Correct))

B) By magnifying the screen and enhancing color contrast

C) By automating mouse movements and clicks

D) By organizing files and folders based on user preferences

Explanation

Option A is correct. The Orca application helps visually impaired users interact with the desktop environment by providing voice feedback for screen content and keyboard input, making it accessible through audio cues.

Question 36:

Add the editor group to the secondary groups of christian. Assume that this group already contains emma, dave, and frank as ordinary members. How can you verify that there are no administrators for this group? Options:

A) cat /etc/group | grep editor

B) grep editor /etc/group

C) getent group editor

((Correct))

D) members editor

Explanation

Option C correctly uses the getent group command to display the details of the editor group, including its members, without distinguishing between ordinary members and administrators.

Question 37:

Run the ls -l /etc/passwd /etc/group /etc/shadow /etc/gshadow command and describe the output that it gives you in terms of file permissions. Which of these four files are shadowed for security reasons? Assume your system uses shadow passwords. Options:

A) /etc/passwd and /etc/group are readable by all users; /etc/shadow and /etc/gshadow are readable only by root.

((**Correct**))

B) /etc/passwd and /etc/group are readable and writable by root only; /etc/shadow and /etc/gshadow are readable by root only.

C) All four files are readable and writable by root only.

D) /etc/passwd and /etc/group are readable by all users; /etc/shadow and /etc/gshadow are readable and writable by root only.

Explanation

Option A accurately describes the file permissions, where /etc/passwd and /etc/group are readable by all users but /etc/shadow and /etc/gshadow are only readable by root, providing enhanced security for sensitive password information.

Question 38:

Without further options or arguments, the command `mail henry@lab3.campus` enters the input mode so the user can type the message to henry@lab3.campus. After finishing the message, which keystroke will close the input mode and dispatch the email? Options:

A) Ctrl + D

((**Correct**))

B) Ctrl + C

C) Esc

D) Ctrl + S

Explanation

Pressing Ctrl + D closes the input mode and sends the email.

Question 39:

Which command can the root user execute to list the undelivered messages that originated on the local system? Options:

A) mailq

((Correct))

B) mailstats

C) postqueue

D) postcat

Explanation

The `mailq` command lists the undelivered messages in the mail queue, which includes those originated from the local system.

Question 40:

How can an unprivileged user use the standard MTA method to automatically forward all of their incoming mail to the address dave@lab2.campus? Options:

A) Edit /etc/aliases and add a forwarding rule

B) Use the `echo` command with `|` to pipe emails to the `sendmail` command

C) Edit the .forward file in the user's home directory

((Correct))

D) Use the `mailx` command with the `-f` option to specify the forwarding address

Explanation

By editing the .forward file in the user's home directory and adding the forwarding address, the user can automatically forward their incoming mail to the specified address.

Question 41:

A new printer was just installed on a local workstation named office-mgr. What command could be used to set this printer as the default for this workstation? Options:

A) `lpadmin -d office-mgr`

((Correct))

B) `lpoptions -d office-mgr`

C) `lp -d office-mgr`

D) `lpoptions -d default=office-mgr`

Explanation

The `lpadmin -d office-mgr` command is used to set the default printer to office-mgr.

Question 42:

Which command and option would be used to determine what printers are available for printing from a workstation? Options:

A) `lpq -a`

B) `lpstat -p`

C) `lpoptions -l`

D) `lpstat -a`

((Correct))

Explanation

The `lpstat -a` command is used to display all available printers.

Question 43:

Using the cancel command, how would you remove a print job with ID 15 that is stuck in the queue for the printer named office-mgr? Options:

A) `cancel 15`

B) `cancel office-mgr 15`

((Correct))

C) `cancel -H office-mgr 15`

D) `cancel -u office-mgr 15`

Explanation

The `cancel` command followed by the printer name and job ID is used to remove a specific print job from the queue.

Question 44:

You have a print job destined for a printer that does not have enough paper to print the full file. What command would you use to move the print job with ID 2 queued to print on the FRONT-DESK printer over to the print queue for the

ACCOUNTING-LASERJET printer? Options:

A) `lpmove 2 ACCOUNTING-LASERJET`

B) `lprm 2 FRONT-DESK`

C) `cancel 2`

D) `lpmove 2 FRONT-DESK ACCOUNTING-LASERJET`
((**Correct**))

Explanation

The `lpmove` command is used to move a print job from one queue to another.

Question 45:

Verify that the CUPS daemon is running, then verify that the PDF printer is enabled and set to the default. Options:

A) `systemctl status cups` and `lpstat -d`

((**Correct**))

B) `service cups status` and `lpq -d`

C) `systemctl status cupsd` and `lpoptions -d`

D) `service cupsd status` and `lpstat -d`

Explanation

`systemctl status cups` checks the status of the CUPS daemon, and `lpstat -d` displays the default printer.

Question 46:

Run a command that will print the /etc/services file. You should now have a directory named PDF within your home directory. Options:

A) `lp -d PDF /etc/services`

B) `lpr -P PDF /etc/services`

((**Correct**))

C) `lp -d PDF -n 1 /etc/services`

D) `lpr -P PDF -n 1 /etc/services`

Explanation

The `-P` option specifies the printer, and `/etc/services` is the file to be printed.

Question 47:

Use a command that will only disable the printer, then run a separate command that shows all status information to verify that the PDF printer is disabled. Then try to print a copy of your /etc/fstab file. What happens? Options:

A) `cupsdisable PDF` and `cupsctl --all-status`

((**Correct**))

B) `cupsdisable PDF` and `cupsctl --list-printers`

C) `lpoptions -d PDF-disabled` and `cupsctl --all-status`

D) `lpoptions -d PDF-disabled` and `cupsctl --list-printers`

Explanation

`cupsdisable PDF` disables the PDF printer, and `cupsctl --all-status` shows all status information.

Question 48:

Now try to print a copy of the /etc/fstab file to the PDF printer. What happens? Options:

A) The print job is successful.

B) The print job is queued but does not complete.

C) An error message is displayed.

((Correct))

D) Nothing happens; the print command fails silently.

Explanation

Since the printer is disabled, attempting to print will result in an error message.

Question 49:

Cancel the print job, then remove the PDF printer. Options:

A) `cancel -a` and `lpadmin -x PDF`

B) `lpq -a` and `lpadmin -r PDF`

((Correct))

C) `cancel -a` and `cupsdisable PDF`

D) `lpq -a` and `cupsdisable PDF`

Explanation

`lpq -a` lists all print jobs, and `lpadmin -r PDF` removes the PDF printer.

Question 50:

How can you force traceroute to use a different interface?

A) `traceroute -i INTERFACE HOST`

((Correct))

B) `traceroute -r INTERFACE HOST`

C) `traceroute -t INTERFACE HOST`

D) `traceroute -f INTERFACE HOST`

Explanation

The `-i` option followed by the interface name allows you to force traceroute to use a specific interface.

Question 51:

Is it possible for traceroute to report MTUs?

A) Yes

((Correct))

B) No

Explanation

Traceroute can report MTUs along the path to a destination if the `-M` option is used.

Question 52:

Which option can be used with the dig command to suppress all output except the result?

A) +short

((Correct))

B) +verbose

C) +quiet

D) +simple

Explanation

The +short option can be used with the dig command to suppress all output except the result.

Question 53:

What is the purpose of the /etc/hosts file in Linux?

A) To configure DNS servers

B) To configure local name resolution

((Correct))

C) To configure network interfaces

D) To configure firewall rules

Explanation

The /etc/hosts file is used to resolve names to IP addresses and vice versa for local name resolution in Linux.

Question 54:

What will the command `getent group openldap` do?

A) Display information about the openldap group

((Correct))

B) Display information about the openldap user

C) Add the openldap group to the system

D) Remove the openldap group from the system

Explanation

The ` getent group ` command retrieves information about the specified group from the system's databases.

Question 55:

What is the biggest difference between getent and the other tools covered, host and dig?

A) getent is used for DNS resolution, while host and dig are used for user/group lookup

B) getent retrieves information from system databases, while host and dig perform DNS queries

((Correct))

C) getent requires root privileges, while host and dig can be used by any user

D) getent works only on Linux systems, while host and dig are cross-platform

Explanation

getent retrieves information from various system databases, while host and dig are used for querying DNS servers.

Question 56:

Which option to dig and host is used to specify the type of record you wish to retrieve?

A) -t

((Correct))

B) -r

C) -q

D) -s

Explanation

The `-t` option is used to specify the type of DNS record you want to retrieve with dig and host commands.

Question 57:

Which of the following is a proper /etc/hosts entry?

::1 localhost

localhost 127.0.0.1

A) ::1 localhost

B) localhost 127.0.0.1

C) Both are proper entries

((Correct))

D) Neither is a proper entry

Explanation

Both entries are commonly used in the /etc/hosts file for mapping the localhost address.

Question 58:

Which option to getent is used to specify which data source should be used to perform a lookup?

A) -s

B) -d

((Correct))

C) -l

D) -u

Explanation

The `-d` option allows you to specify which database to use when performing a lookup with getent.

Question 59:

If you were to edit the /etc/resolv.conf below with a text editor, what is likely to happen?

 # Generated by NetworkManager

nameserver 192.168.1.20

A) The changes will be overwritten by NetworkManager.

((Correct))

B) NetworkManager will update its configuration with your changes.

C) Your changes won't affect the system.

D) NetworkManager will be disabled.

Explanation

NetworkManager often manages the /etc/resolv.conf file, and any manual changes made to it are typically overwritten by NetworkManager.

Question 60:

What does the following line in /etc/nsswitch.conf mean:

`hosts: files [SUCCESS=continue] dns`

A) The system first checks the files database for host information, then continues to DNS if successful.

((Correct))

B) The system checks both the files and DNS databases simultaneously.

C) The system only checks the files database for host information and continues to DNS regardless of success.

D) The system prioritizes DNS over the files database for host information.

Explanation

This line specifies the lookup order for host information, starting with the files database and continuing to DNS if the files lookup is successful.

Question 61:

Considering the following /etc/resolv.conf why isn't the system resolving names through DNS?

search lpi.org

#nameserver fd00:ffff::1:53

#nameserver 10.0.1.53

A) DNS servers are commented out

((Correct))

B) Incorrect DNS server IP addresses

C) Missing domain name

D) Missing search directive

Explanation

Both nameserver lines are commented out (prefixed with #), meaning the DNS servers are not being used.

Question 62:

What does the command dig +noall +answer +question lpi.org do?

A) Displays all DNS records for lpi.org domain

B) Displays only the question and answer sections for DNS lookup of lpi.org

((Correct))

C) Displays only the question section for DNS lookup of lpi.org

D) Displays only the answer section for DNS lookup of lpi.org

Explanation

The `+noall` option disables all display sections, and `+answer` and `+question` options enable the answer and question sections, respectively.

Question 63:

How can you override the defaults of dig without specifying them on the command line?

A) Set environment variables

B) Edit /etc/dig.conf

C) Use aliases

D) Use a configuration file

((Correct))

Explanation

You can use a configuration file to set defaults for dig without specifying them on the command line.

Question 64:

Which option to `getent` is used to specify which data source should be used to perform a lookup?

A) -d

B) -s

((Correct))

C) -f

D) -g

Explanation

The `-s` option in `getent` is used to specify the database or data source to perform the lookup.

Question 65:

You have installed the nginx web server. How can you check whether nginx supports TCPwrappers?

A) Use the `nginx -v` command and check for TCPwrappers support in the output.

B) Inspect the /etc/nginx/nginx.conf file for a TCPwrappers directive.

C) Use the `nginx -V` command and inspect the output for TCPwrappers support.

((**Correct**))

D) Check the /etc/hosts.allow and /etc/hosts.deny files for nginx entries.

Explanation

The `nginx -V` command shows the compile-time options, including whether TCPwrappers support is enabled.

Question 66:

Which option is used to sign a file using GPG?

A) --encrypt

B) --verify

C) --sign

((**Correct**))

D) --decrypt

Explanation

The `--sign` option is used to sign a file using GPG.

Question 67:

What is the purpose of verifying a signature in GPG?

A) To ensure the file is not encrypted

B) To confirm the authenticity of the file

((**Correct**))

C) To decrypt the file contents

D) To compress the file for storage

Explanation

Verifying a signature in GPG confirms that the file has not been tampered with and originates from the expected source.

Question 68:

How can a revoked private key be made unavailable for further use in GPG?

A) By deleting the private key file

B) By removing the corresponding public key

C) By importing the revocation certificate

((Correct))

D) By changing the passphrase

Explanation

Importing the revocation certificate into GPG marks the private key as revoked and makes it unavailable for further use.

Question 69:

What is the purpose of the GPG-Agent in GPG encryption?

A) To manage private keys

((Correct))

B) To encrypt files

C) To distribute public keys

D) To revoke keys

Explanation

The GPG-Agent is responsible for managing private keys in GPG encryption.

Question 70:

Which command is used to decrypt an encrypted message in GPG?

A) gpg --decrypt

((Correct))

B) gpg --open

C) gpg --unencrypt

D) gpg --decode

Explanation

The `gpg --decrypt` command is used to decrypt an encrypted message in GPG.

Question 71:

Check if the provided filenames are correct. These filenames correspond to specific components of the GnuPG (GPG) cryptographic system, each serving a distinct purpose in managing keys and trust:

- Trust database: *trustdb.gpg*

- Directory for revocation certificates: *.gnupg/openpgp-revocs.d*

- Directory for private keys: *.gnupg/private-keys-v1.d*

- Public keyring: *pubring.gpg*

A) True

((**Correct**))

B) False

Explanation

The correct answer is: True

trustdb.gpg: This file stores the trust database, which contains information about the level of trust assigned to different keys.

.gnupg/openpgp-revocs.d: This directory stores revocation certificates, which are used to revoke public keys.

.gnupg/private-keys-v1.d: This directory stores private keys, each stored in a separate file, allowing GnuPG to manage them efficiently.

pubring.gpg: This file represents the public keyring, which contains public keys of trusted contacts.

These filenames are correct and correspond to essential components of the GnuPG cryptographic system, aiding in key management, trust establishment, and secure communication.

Understanding the purpose and location of these files is crucial for managing keys and trust in the GnuPG system, ensuring the security and integrity of cryptographic operations.

Question 72:

What type of cryptography is used by GnuPG?

A) Symmetric-key cryptography

B) Asymmetric-key cryptography

((Correct))

C) Hash-based cryptography

D) Stream cipher cryptography

Explanation

GnuPG (GPG) uses asymmetric-key cryptography, also known as public-key cryptography.

Question 73:

What are the two main components of public key cryptography?

A) Private key and passphrase

B) Key ID and fingerprint

C) Public key and private key

((Correct))

D) Encryption and decryption algorithms

Explanation

Public key cryptography involves a pair of keys: a public key for encryption and a private key for decryption.

Question 74:

What is the KEY-ID of the public key fingerprint 07A6 5898 2D3A F3DD 43E3 DA95 1F3F 3147 FA7F 54C7?

A) 07A6 5898

B) 3147 FA7F

((Correct))

C) 1F3F 54C7

D) DA95 43E3

Explanation

In the given fingerprint, the last 8 characters represent the KEY-ID.

Question 75:

What method is used to distribute public keys at a global level?

A) Public Key Infrastructure (PKI)

B) Certificate Revocation Lists (CRL)

C) Web of Trust (WoT)

((Correct))

D) Certificate Authorities (CA)

Explanation

The Web of Trust (WoT) is a decentralized method used to distribute and verify public keys at a global level.

Question 76:

Confirm if the following steps concerning private key revocation are in the right order:

1. Create a revocation certificate.

2. Import the revocation certificate to your keyring.

3. Make the revoked key available to your correspondents.

A) Yes

((**Correct**))

B) No

Explanation

To properly revoke a private key, the following steps should be taken in order:

1. Create a revocation certificate, which serves as a formal statement that the key should no longer be trusted.

2. Import the revocation certificate to your keyring, ensuring that your system recognizes the key as revoked.

3. Share the revoked key and its corresponding revocation certificate with your correspondents, informing them that the key is no longer valid and should not be used for further communication.

Question 77:

Regarding file encryption, what does the --armor option imply in the command ` gpg --output encrypted-message --recipient carol --armor --encrypt unencrypted message ` ?

A) It specifies the recipient's name.

B) It encrypts the message with ASCII armor.

((**Correct**))

C) It signs the message with the sender's private key.

D) It compresses the message before encryption.

Explanation

The `--armor` option instructs GPG to create ASCII-armored output, which is base64-encoded encrypted data that can be safely sent via email or other text-based channels.

Question 78:

Which of the following commands is used to schedule recurring tasks in Linux?

A) cron

((Correct))

B) at

C) task

D) sched

Explanation

The `cron` command is used to schedule recurring tasks in Linux by setting up cron jobs.

Question 79:

What is the purpose of the `tar` command in Linux?

A) Compress files

B) Copy files

C) Extract files from an archive

((Correct))

D) Encrypt files

Explanation

While `tar` can be used for various purposes, its primary

function is to create, maintain, modify, and extract files from archives.

Question 80:

Which of the following filesystems is commonly used in Linux and supports journaling for improved reliability?

A) FAT32

B) NTFS

C) ext4

((**Correct**))

D) HFS+

Explanation

ext4 is a commonly used filesystem in Linux distributions and supports journaling for enhanced reliability and faster crash recovery.

Question 81:

What is the purpose of the `grep` command in Linux?

A) Search for text patterns in files

((**Correct**))

B) Copy files

C) Move files

D) Remove files

Explanation

The `grep` command is used to search for specific text

patterns within files or streams in Linux.

Question 82:

Which of the following commands is used to display the contents of a file in reverse order in Linux?

A) cat

B) more

C) tail

D) tac

((Correct))

Explanation

The `tac` command is similar to `cat` but displays the contents of a file in reverse order, line by line.

Question 83:

You have a shell script that takes a filename as input. You need to make the script extract just the filename (without the directory path) from the provided input. Which of the following commands would accomplish this?

A) echo $filename | cut -d '/' -f1

B) dirname $filename

C) head -n1 $filename

D) basename $filename

((Correct))

Explanation

echo $filename | cut -d '/' -f1 would give you the first field if delimited by "/", but might not be the filename if the path is complex.

dirname $filename extracts the directory portion of the path, not the filename.

head -n1 $filename outputs the first line of the file's contents, not the filename itself.

basename $filename is a utility specifically designed to strip directory information and output the filename.

Question 84:

You want to configure a web server to start automatically when your Linux system boots. Which of the following commands (or tools) would you likely use?

A) crontab

B) systemctl enable httpd.service (or service httpd start)

((Correct))

C) inittab

D) at

Explanation

crontab is used for scheduling tasks, not managing system services at boot.

systemctl (for systemd-based systems) or service (for older systems) are used to manage system services, including enabling/disabling them at startup.

inittab is used on legacy SysV init systems, not as common in modern distributions.

at is for scheduling tasks for one-time execution, not for managing startup services.

Question 85:

You need to temporarily set a static IP address of 192.168.1.100 with a netmask of 255.255.255.0 on interface eth0. Which command accomplishes this?

A) route add default gw 192.168.1.1 eth0

B) ifconfig eth0 192.168.1.100 netmask 255.255.255.0

C) ip addr add 192.168.1.100/24 dev eth0

((Correct))

D) dhclient eth0

Explanation

route add default gw... configures a default gateway, not a static IP.

ifconfig is used in older systems, while ip is the modern tool.

Using /24 subnet notation with ip addr sets the right netmask.

dhclient automates IP address assignment via DHCP, not for static configuration.

Question 86:

Which configuration file stores the IP addresses of the DNS servers that your system uses for name resolution?

A) /etc/hosts

B) /etc/resolv.conf

((Correct))

C) /etc/hostname

D) /etc/nsswitch.conf

Explanation

- */etc/hosts* provides static hostname to IP mappings.

- */etc/resolv.conf* lists DNS servers your system queries for resolving addresses.

- */etc/hostname* only contains your system's hostname

- */etc/nsswitch.conf* determines the order in which services (like DNS) are consulted.

Question 87:

Which of the following commands will change the ownership of a file?

A) chown

((Correct))

B) chmod

C) chgrp

D) chuser

Explanation

The chown command in Linux is used to change the owner of a file or directory. The chmod command changes the permissions of a file or directory, chgrp changes the group ownership, and chuser is not a valid command.

Question 88:

Which of the following commands can be used to view the contents of a compressed file without decompressing it?

A) cat

B) zcat

((**Correct**))

C) less

D) more

Explanation

The zcat command in Linux is used to view the contents of a compressed file without decompressing it. The cat, less, and more commands can be used to view the contents of a file, but they do not work with compressed files without the help of other commands.

Question 89:

Which of the following commands will display the last part of a file?

A) head

B) tail

((**Correct**))

C) cat

D) less

Explanation

The tail command in Linux is used to display the last part of a file. The head command displays the first part of a file, and the cat and less commands can be used to view the entire contents of a file.

Question 90:

Which command would allow a user named "john" to create files and directories owned by the "accounting" group, without changing the default group for new files created by "john"?

A) newgrp accounting

B) chgrp accounting /home/john

C) usermod -a -G accounting john

((Correct))

D) chown accounting /home/john

Explanation

- *newgrp accounting* would temporarily switch "john" to the "accounting" group, but doesn't affect future file ownership.

- *chgrp accounting /home/john* would change the group ownership of the existing "/home/john" directory, but it won't affect newly created files.

- *usermod -a -G accounting john* adds the "accounting" group to "john"'s supplementary groups, allowing newly created files to have "accounting" as the group owner while preserving "john"'s default group.

- *chown accounting /home/john* would change both the owner and group ownership of the "/home/john" directory, not ideal for ongoing file ownership.

EPILOGUE

Congratulations! You've reached the culmination of your journey through "LPIC-1 102-500 V5 Exam Prep: Master Linux Admin with 6 Practice Tests." By diligently working through the practice exams, mastering the key concepts, and leveraging the provided resources, you've equipped yourself with the essential knowledge and skills to confidently approach the LPIC-1 exam.

Remember, the LPIC-1 certification is merely the first step on your exciting path to becoming a proficient Linux administrator. The world of Linux is vast and continuously evolving. Embrace the spirit of lifelong learning:

- **Engage in online communities:** Connect with fellow Linux enthusiasts and professionals, share knowledge, ask questions, and collaborate on projects.
- **Contribute to open-source:** Immerse yourself in the collaborative spirit by contributing to existing projects or even starting your own.
- **Stay updated:** The Linux landscape is dynamic, so make it a habit to stay informed about new developments and emerging tools.
- **Explore further certifications:** As your skills and knowledge expand, consider pursuing advanced Linux certifications to enhance your career prospects.

The key to success in this field lies in your passion for learning and your commitment to continuous improvement. I wish you the very best of luck in your LPIC-1 exam and your future endeavors in the ever-evolving realm of Linux administration!

GHADA ATEF

ABOUT THE AUTHOR

Ghada Atef: Empowering Linux Explorers

Ghada Atef, a seasoned Linux expert, breathes life into the command line. Her passion for open-source technologies fuels her journey across various Linux distributions. With unwavering dedication, she has crafted a constellation of resources to illuminate the path for aspiring Linux professionals:

1. "RHCSA 9 (EX200) Exam Prep": The third edition of this comprehensive guide unveils six complete practice exams—a compass for RHCSA 9 (EX200) certification seekers.
2. "Mastering Ansible": Ghada dives deep into Ansible, revealing practical insights on automating configuration management and deployment.
3. "Ubuntu Mastery": Her in-depth exploration of Ubuntu—the beloved Linux distribution—equips learners with mastery.
4. "RHCSA 8 & 9 Exam Prep": Ghada's meticulous preparation guide, including six practice exams, readies candidates for RHCSA 8 & 9 (EX200).
5. "RHCE EX294 Mastery": Here, detailed answers and strategic wisdom converge, paving the way to excellence in the Red Hat Certified Engineer EX294 Exam.

Her work transcends theory—practicality reigns supreme.

Clear explanations, real-world relevance, and a dash of Linux magic define her legacy. Whether you're a curious beginner or a seasoned pro, Ghada's books and courses are your compass in the vast Linux wilderness.

Embark on this journey. Let the terminal echo your footsteps.

BOOKS BY THIS AUTHOR

Unofficial Rhcsa 8 & 9 (Ex200) Complete Reference: Rhel 8 & 9

"Unofficial RHCSA 8 & 9 (EX200) Complete Reference: RHEL 8 & 9" is a comprehensive guide that covers all the topics and objectives of the Red Hat Certified System Administrator (RHCSA) exam for RHEL 8 and 9. Whether you're a beginner or an experienced Linux user, this book provides you with the knowledge and skills to become proficient in managing and maintaining RHEL systems. From installation and configuration to system management, networking, security, and troubleshooting, this book covers everything you need to know to pass the RHCSA exam and become a certified system administrator. With clear explanations, practical examples, and real-world scenarios, "Unofficial RHCSA 8 & 9 (EX200) Complete Reference: RHEL 8 & 9" is an essential resource for anyone preparing for the RHCSA exam or seeking to improve their RHEL skills.

Mastering Ansible: A Comprehensive Guide To Automating Configuration Management And Deployment

"Mastering Ansible: A Comprehensive Guide to Automating Configuration Management and Deployment" is an in-depth guide to Ansible, a popular open-source tool for automating infrastructure as code.

The book covers everything from the basics of Ansible to advanced topics such as modules, plugins, roles, and dynamic inventory. It provides detailed guidance on how to write efficient, modular, and reusable playbooks, and how to use Ansible to automate a wide range of tasks, from provisioning servers to deploying applications.

The book also includes best practices, tips, and tricks for working effectively with Ansible, as well as use cases and real-world examples.

Whether you're a beginner or an experienced user, "Mastering Ansible" will help you become a master of Ansible and take your automation skills to the next level.

Unofficial Red Hat Certified Engineer (Rhce) Ex294 Exam Guide: A Comprehensive Study Resource For Red Hat Enterprise Linux 9

Looking to become a Red Hat Certified Engineer (RHCE)? Look no further than "Unofficial Red Hat Certified Engineer (RHCE) EX294 Exam Guide"! This comprehensive study resource is designed to help you pass the RHCE EX294 exam with ease, providing in-depth coverage of all exam objectives and six complete practice exams to help you sharpen your skills. With its clear explanations, helpful tips, and real-world scenarios, this book is an essential tool for anyone looking to succeed on the RHCE EX294 exam and take their Linux skills to the next level. So why wait? Get your copy today and start preparing for exam success!

Mastering Ubuntu: A Comprehensive Guide To Linux's Favorite Distribution

Looking to master one of the most popular Linux distributions around? Look no further than "Mastering Ubuntu"! This comprehensive guide takes you on a journey from beginner to expert, with step-by-step tutorials and practical examples to help you get the most out of your Ubuntu system. Whether you're a developer, sysadmin, or just a curious user, "Mastering Ubuntu" has everything you need to take your skills to the next level. From installation and configuration to networking, security, and beyond, this book is your ultimate resource for mastering Ubuntu.

Learn Pycharm Ide For Kids: Using Pycharm Python Ide Community Edition

Looking for a fun and engaging way to introduce your child to the world of programming? Look no further than "Learn PyCharm IDE for Kids: Using PyCharm Python IDE Community Edition." This book offers a comprehensive guide to the PyCharm Python IDE, one of the most popular tools for programming in Python. With clear and easy-to-follow instructions, your child will learn how to use PyCharm to write and run Python code, as well as how to debug and troubleshoot their programs. Whether your child is a complete beginner or has some programming experience, "Learn PyCharm IDE for Kids" is the perfect resource to help them take their coding skills to the next level.

Unofficial Red Hat Rhcsa 9 (Ex200) Exam Preparation 2023: Six Complete Rhcsa 9 (Ex200) Practice Exams With Answers (Third Edition)

Looking to ace the Red Hat RHCSA 9 (EX200) exam? Look no further than the "Unofficial Red Hat RHCSA 9 (EX200) Exam Preparation 2023" book. With six complete practice exams for RHCSA 9, this book is the ultimate study resource for anyone preparing to take the RHCSA exam. Whether you're a beginner or an experienced professional, these practice exams will test your knowledge and skills, giving you the confidence you need to pass the RHCSA exam with flying colors. With answers and detailed explanations included, you'll be able to review and strengthen your understanding of key concepts, commands, and techniques. Don't take the RHCSA exam without this essential study guide!

Rhce Ex294 Mastery: Six Practice Exams For Exam Success

This book, "RHCE EX294 Mastery: Six Practice Exams for Exam Success," is your comprehensive guide to achieving RHCE certification. It provides the tools, strategies, and in-depth knowledge to confidently ace the RHCE EX294 exam and establish yourself as a true RHEL expert.

Command Line Mastery

A Comprehensive Guide to Linux and Bash: 615 MCQs with detailed explanations on Filesystem, Process Management, Permissions, Networking, and Bash Scripting

THANK YOU!

www.ingramcontent.com/pod-product-compliance
Lightning Source LLC
LaVergne TN
LVHW051221050326
832903LV00028B/2194